PACIFIC NORTHWEST

A Photographic Journey

TEXT: **Suzi Forbes**

CAPTIONS: **Pauline Graham**

DESIGNED BY: **Teddy Hartshorn**

EDITORIAL: **Gill Waugh and Pauline Graham**

PRODUCTION: **Ruth Arthur and David Proffit**

DIRECTOR OF PRODUCTION: **Gerald Hughes**

DIRECTOR OF PUBLISHING: **David Gibbon**

CLB 2442
© 1989 Colour Library Books Ltd., Godalming, Surrey, England.
All rights reserved.
This 1989 edition published by Crescent Books,
distributed by Crown Publishers, Inc., 225 Park Avenue South, New York, New York 10003.
Printed and bound in Hong Kong.
ISBN 0 517 00174 8
h g f e d c b a

PACIFIC NORTHWEST

A Photographic Journey

Text by
SUZI FORBES

CRESCENT BOOKS

NEW YORK

Jack Pennington has climbed Mount Rainier eight times. He has backpacked the Pacific Crest Trail from the Canadian border to Mount Shasta in California. He's lean and trim and tan. Now he's in training for the big one. He's determined to climb Mt. Everest. He's not alone among Pacific Northwesterners. In fact, it seems to be an obsession with many folks who live there. They're a rugged, outdoors lot who count fishing, hiking, hunting, climbing, boating, backpacking, sailing, camping and skiing among their pastimes.

Jack wasn't raised in the Pacific Northwest. He actually grew up in New York City. Maybe the mountains remind him of all those tall buildings back home. How did he ever find his way to Seattle? It's a common tale – heard over and over. After graduation from high school, Jack was offered a football scholarship to three pretty good schools. Two were on the East Coast and the other was in the town of Corvallis, Oregon. Oregon State, it was called. Why not see the country, thought Jack. He'd never been beyond the Mississippi River. So there he was in Corvallis, Oregon, and loving every minute of it. He just never left – except to climb another mountain, that is.

Of all the folks living in the Pacific Northwest more than half came from somewhere else. And even after arriving in the Northwest, they seem to move around more than their Eastern cousins. In fact, one in three families changes residences every year compared to one in five in the rest of the United States. Each place they visit just looks that much better than the last. Once they find the Pacific Northwest, though, they seldom leave the area.

It's a land of contrasts and of contentment. It's an abrupt land, where waves crash against the shore, creating jagged cliffs and rocky promontories. Where cliffs surge out of the sea onto flat mesas that give way in turn to valleys and hills. The mountains are always there in the background, like the backdrop to a stageset. Rushing rivers create fertile valleys. It's a land of abundance. And it's not called "God's Country" for nothing.

But it's a recent discovery to the white man. Although Balboa discovered the Pacific Ocean in 1533, another 250 years went by before Captain Cook, sailing under the British flag, accomplished what amounted to exploration of the Pacific Northwest coast. We pay attention to what he says because he had the training and foresight to write it down. Legend has it, however, that a strait leading into a large and peaceful body of water had once been discovered by a Greek sailor named Valerianos, who called himself Juan de Fuca, many years earlier. The strait still bears his name. We also know that Juan Perez of Spain visited many points on Oregon's coast in 1744.

Nevertheless, it is Captain Cook we credit. In 1778, Cook skittered northward from the South Pacific, where he had languished in the sun for eighteen months. On his way North, he found the Sandwich Islands (Hawaii) and then reached the Oregon Coast in March. Sailing ever further northward, he landed in Nootka Sound on present-day Vancouver Island, where friendly Indians offered him furs. Still traveling north, he eventually sailed through the Bering Strait separating Alaska from Russia. He called it "the western extremity of all America." Cook returned to the Sandwich Islands where he infuriated the native Hawaiians. Seems he chopped up a temple to provide firewood for his ship. No more sailing for Cook. He lost his life at their hands.

But his men and ships continued on to China – Canton to be exact – to sell their wares. Much to their surprise, they found the furs to be their most popular item. "Skins which did not cost the purchaser sixpence sterling," wrote one man, "sold for one hundred dollars." That did it. They couldn't wait to

return to the Pacific Northwest to pick up another load.

In no time at all, ships from England, Portugal, Spain, France and even the foundling republic of the United States were flying back and forth with their precious cargos of furs – especially the highly prized otter skins.

England sent one of her foremost geographers to explore and map the region so new to them all. Captain George Vancouver spent the better part of three summers exploring inlets, sounds and rivers from San Diego in California to Cook's Inlet in Alaska – always searching for the Northwest Passage. In between, he explored the great inland sea that the Strait of Juan de Fuca leads a path to – calling it Puget Sound after his friend, Lieutenant Peter Puget. He circumnavigated the enormous island that he named Vancouver Island and he charted the California, Oregon, Washington and British Columbia coasts.

These discoveries were only the beginning. Because the fur trade was increasing in importance, countries sent their best explorers to research it. Traders learned they could get the best prices from Indians who had never seen a white man. This led to more innovative explorations and finally, in May, 1792, Captain Robert Gray, in his little ship *Columbia* frisked across the breakers into the mouth of a giant river. He traveled about thirty miles inland, trading with the Indians along the way. He named the mighty river after his ship, calling it the Columbia River.

Gray was an American and his voyage opened new horizons for a new country that had only recently won its freedom from Great Britain. Gray's ship had been fitted out and financed in Boston. On his first trip he collected over 700 otter skins on the Pacific Coast and then sold them in China. It seems that men thrilled to the sight of these lovely silver furs tipped with white – and to the price they brought. One trader is said to have expressed the sentiment that "except for a beautiful woman and a lovely infant" an otter skin was the most beautiful object he had ever seen.

When Gray returned to Boston from his second voyage, he brought a handsome profit for his backers. In fact, it is reputed that the *Columbia* did so well that by 1804 there were over fifty ships occupied on the "China Trade" from Boston to the Northwest, to the Sandwich Islands and then to China and back to Boston. During the years 1801-1802 more than 15,000 sea otter skins were collected. Profit on one voyage alone was 90,000 dollars and on another, 234,000 dollars. Not bad for two years work in 1804.

Meanwhile, although Daniel Boone had led his band of settlers into Kentucky's wilderness in 1769, not much had been done about penetrating the land beyond. In fact, it wasn't until 1793 that anyone thought much about establishing an overland route to the Pacific Ocean. But in that year Alexander Mackenzie did more than just think about it.

Mackenzie was involved in the Canadian fur trade, but not as an associate of the indomitable Hudson's Bay Company. He was a partner in a young upstart called the North West Company. The two companies were bitter rivals and Mackenzie believed that by establishing a fur route across the breadth of Canada his company would prosper. It was not a bad idea.

He set out with ten woodsmen and a store of provisions. They traveled over land by foot and down rivers by boat. His resolve intensified when he found a westerly flowing river. He followed it, finding himself in the Fraser River. This empties into Puget Sound near present-day Vancouver, British Columbia. Actually, he thought it was the Columbia River, mapped earlier by Gray. What disappointment he felt when he realized his error! Nevertheless, it's clear that it was a Canadian who first made the cross-country trek and established an overland route to the Pacific Coast.

Thomas Jefferson was President of the United States by now. Curiosity about lands beyond his home had earlier led him to become Minister of France and he traveled widely throughout Europe. He loved problems of every sort. He was restless to learn the unknown, especially about the great nation he had helped to found and was now leader of. He admitted that "the works of nature in the large" were especially fascinating to him and he longed to learn more about the mountains, rivers and geographic masses of his continent.

And so, in January 1803, Jefferson sent a message to Congress recommending an exploring expedition to the Pacific. He said: "An intelligent officer, with ten or twelve men fit for the enterprise, and willing to undertake it, might explore the whole line, even to the Western Ocean, have conferences with the natives on the subject of commercial intercourse, get admission among them for our traders, as others are admitted, agree on a convenient deposit for an interchange of articles, and return with the information acquired in the course of two summers."

Meriwether Lewis, then twenty-nine years old, was secretary to President Jefferson. It seems he had known Jefferson for some time, having been raised near Jefferson's home of Monticello in Virginia. He asked if he might lead the expedition. Jefferson thought it was a splendid idea.

Although Lewis had never been west, it had always been his fondest hope to do so. He seems outwardly to have been an unlikely candidate – a shy, moody man – even awkward. Yet he found that the challenge of nature met his innermost needs.

He had always loved to hunt and was a supreme woodsman. Furthermore, he had been in the regular army and was familiar with the discipline required of such an expedition. Jefferson said of Lewis that he was "honest, disinterested, of sound understanding, and fidelity to truth so scrupulous that whatever he should report would be as certain as if seen by ourselves." He also observed that he was "steady in the maintenance of discipline" and would be "careful as a father of those committed to his charge."

Lewis chose William Clark as his partner. Clark, unlike Lewis, was an outgoing, friendly, affable man, who seems to have understood nature on its own terms. A practical man, he was up to any challenge of man or nature.

Clark was a military man as well. He had traveled in the West, first participating in the campaign against the Ohio Indians and then exploring on his own, even crossing the Mississippi River several times.

Jefferson's instructions were to "explore the Missouri River and such principal stream of it as, by its course and communication with the waters of the Pacific Ocean, whether the Columbia, Oregon, Colorado or some other river, may offer the most direct and practical water communication across the continent for the purpose of commerce." They were still looking for that elusive Northwest Passage.

The President insisted on strict record-keeping and instructed them to note everything; from birds, flowers and wildlife to the important locations of rivers and mountains. He even suggested they make several copies of their notes to guard against the only record being lost to the elements. He urged all the men to keep individual diaries of their personal observations, and some did.

As to the Indians they would encounter, Jefferson instructed the explorers to "treat them in the most friendly and conciliatory manner which their own conduct will admit." He even suggested they might want to arrange to have several influential chiefs visit Washington.

Finally, Jefferson's instructions about their own safety, say much for the great man. He said, "We wish you to err on the side of your safety, and to bring back your party safe, even if it be with less information."

On May 14, 1804, a party of twenty-three set out from St. Louis, then an outpost frontier and the center of the fur trade. Lewis brought his dog and Clark brought his slave. They added a fiddle for song and laughter around the campfire.

The men accompanying Lewis and Clark were military men too – a shrewd move on Jefferson's part because this meant the military paid their salaries. They were lean and tough and used to a rough but disciplined life.

On May 25th, they passed La Charette, the home of Daniel Boone and the last settlement on the Missouri. From here on, it was open space. As they traveled, they found buffalo abounding in great herds. Buffalo meat and buffalo stew satisfied the hungry men as they sat around the campfire at night.

It took them five months to reach their winter camp near present-day Bismarck, North Dakota. A lucky discovery, however, resulted in an addition to their expedition that made the rest of the trip more fun and less dangerous. A middle-aged French-Canadian named Charbonneau, knew the language of several of the Indian tribes they would encounter along the way. They asked him to join their expedition as interpreter. His seventeen-year-old wife, Sacagawea, was familiar with the land they would be crossing. She was a Shoshone princess, who had been kidnapped four years earlier and even knew of "the pass through the mountains." Before the band moved on in April, 1805, Sacagawea had given birth to a baby boy, who became the darling of the camp.

Soon they were passing through vast plains near the mouth of the Yellowstone. They wrote that they were "animated by vast herds of buffalo, deer, elk, and antelope." The animals were so friendly they "often followed quietly for some distance." The grizzly bears, of course, exhibited no fear of the explorers. Indeed, on one occasion, Captain Lewis turned around to find a snarling beast rushing pell-mell toward him. He raced for the river bank, jumped in and somehow missed being torn to pieces.

On they pressed through fields and mountains, fording streams and traveling by river. They finally reached the land of the Shoshone Indians.

No one was happier than Sacagawea. She began to dance "and show every mark of the most extravagant joy..." Not only had she found her people again, but it turned out that the chief was her brother. The Shoshone were pleased to help. They provided horses and guides through the treacherous mountain pass. Without them, Lewis and Clark might not have been able to complete their journey.

They climbed mountains higher than they had ever imagined, sometimes with sheer rocky faces, and passed through forests so dense that they couldn't see one another. They built canoes to carry them down the rivers, passing from the Salmon to the Snake and then to the Columbia that Gray had earlier explored from its mouth. On November 15, 1805, Lewis, Clark and their entourage saw the peaceful waves of the Pacific Ocean lapping against the sandy shore. They had traversed a continent!

They spent the winter on the coast near present-day Seaside, Oregon – naming the outpost Fort Clatsop. All winter it rained. They erected shelters to protect themselves from the cold and wet, but these were inadequate. Food was perilously low. On Christmas Day 1805, Captain Clark wrote: "Some rain at different times last night and showers of hail with intervales of fair starr light...The day proved showery all day...Our Store of Meat entirely Spoiled...Our Dinner to day consisted of poor Elk boiled, spoiled fish and some roots."

They made the return trip in the spring of 1806, reaching St. Louis again on September 23, 1806. They were lucky. During the entire two-and-a-half year expedition, they lost only one man, and that was probably due to appendicitis.

Perhaps we can credit Lewis with this remarkable record. It seems that he was consistently cautious in his approach to danger and refused to take unnecessary risks. But, in addition, he had taken whole satchels of herbs, twigs and powders along. Whenever anyone even hinted of ill health, he forced bitter broths down their throats – an old remedy he had learned from his mother. But it worked.

A grateful President Jefferson and Congress gave both Lewis and Clark 1,600 acres of land and generously rewarded the rest of the men with 320 acres and doubled their pay.

Why all the interest in establishing a route to the Pacific Ocean? Jefferson's interest in nature and knowledge undoubtedly played a role. On the other hand, he was a shrewd politician and an ardent pacifist who realized that by laying claim to these vast territories before someone else did, he could preserve them for the United States. And anyway, he had just arranged the Louisiana Purchase, which included all the land to present-day Idaho on the North and to Texas on the South. He visualized whole new territories opening up for commerce, especially in the fur trade.

Meanwhile, there was much speculation about the new land that had just been explored. Jefferson himself asked a traveler going West to check out a report that "the Lama or Paca of Peru is found in those parts of this continent..."

Men have sought the Northwest Passage for so long that it was difficult to set aside the myth of a great river that flowed east to west. They even had a name for it – the Oregon River. These myths died a hard death, even after Lewis and Clark returned. Somewhere out there the "River of the West" must lead directly to the Pacific. The search continued.

The race for trade dominance of the Oregon country, as it was called, intensified. The North West Company, stimulated by news of the Lewis and Clark expedition, established a trading post in the Rocky Mountains. In 1807, Simon Fraser descended the river that bears his name and founded a post where it empties into Puget Sound. His disappointment was intense when he realized that he had fallen into the same trap as Alexander Mackenzie in 1793. The river he thought was the Columbia, was actually several hundred miles north of that mighty river. The North West Company, straining every effort to stave off an American occupation, pressed on.

Enterprise was equally creative in the United States. Men such as John Jacob Astor had watched the Lewis and Clark expedition with special interest. Astor had been engaged in the fur trade for several years, and he knew that at least seventy-five percent of the furs that entered the United States came from Canada. He operated a fleet of ships out of New York to China. It galled him to buy his furs from such companies as the North West Company and the Hudson's Bay Company in Canada. So, in 1808, he secured a charter from President Jefferson and organized a new company to operate out of New York. He called it the Pacific Fur Company.

Astor sent an overland party and, as custom demanded, they set out on their adventure from St. Louis. Again, as with Lewis and Clark, the last view of civilization they had was of Charette, Daniel Boone's home. There, according to a Mr. Bradbury in his book *Travels in America*, was the great man, standing on the bank of the river. Bradbury recalls: "On leaving Charette, Mr. Hunt pointed out to me an old man standing on the bank, who he informed me was Daniel Boone, the discoverer of Kentucky. As I had a letter of introduction to him from his nephew, Colonel Grant, I went ashore to speak to him...I remained for some time in conversation with him. He informed me that he was eighty-four years of age; that he had spent a considerable portion of his time alone in the backwoods, and had lately returned from his spring hunt with nearly sixty beaver skins."

The Astor party followed a route that would later become the Oregon Trail, arriving at the mouth of the Columbia River in January 1812. The overland expedition was met by a seagoing contingent, also sent by Astor, which had arrived in March 1811. The sailors had experienced untold obstacles. Bickering and anger characterized the sea journey. On arriving at the mouth of the Columbia, Captain Thorn lost six of his men when their small boat capsized while searching for the channel across the bar. A pall hung over the survivors on the ship.

Thorn landed, left a group on shore to establish a fort and immediately set out again by ship to gather otter pelts. Although the Indians had been friendly, Thorn had a terrible temper and, angered by the Indians' prices (seems they had learned to barter) he struck an Indian chief with a stick.

Things simply went from bad to worse. The Indians boarded Thorn's ship and slaughtered most on board – all except for five sailors who had been in the riggings. When they could finally skuttle down, they barricaded themselves in the storehouse. During the night four of the five escaped. Next morning, when the Indians boarded the ship again to take away their spoils, a giant explosion occurred, killing at least 200 Indians. It is presumed that the one remaining sailor had ignited the powder kegs, taking his own life rather than allowing the ship and goods to be claimed by the Indians.

It was an ominous start for Astor's Pacific Fur Trading Company. Left alone in this abandoned outpost that they called "Astoria" the men became discouraged and depressed. Not until May, 1812, did the supply ship *Beaver* show up, bringing nails, liquor, food, clothing and fresh courage. Seems it was the liquor they needed the most. The Indians had become used to their "firewater."

Not to be outdone by their American cousins, the Canadians never gave up. David Thompson finally paddled down the elusive Columbia River to its mouth in 1811, only to be met by the stars and stripes flying from the crude fort at Astoria. Actually, Astor had recruited his men from the North West Company, so Thompson met other Canadians working for an American Company. This must have been especially painful to him.

Trade progressed with the Indians and the establishment called Astoria flourished. But not for long. When news reached Astoria in 1813 that the United States was at war with Great Britain again, Astorians feared the worst. The North West Company was able to convince the British that their interests in the Pacific region must be secured. The British Admiralty promised to send naval support. Neither the United States government nor Astor were able to defend their claim. When news came that a British man-of-war would be arriving shortly, plans were made to sell Astoria – fur, supplies, fort and all.

The North West Company was eager to buy. Why wait for the British man-of-war and allow the fort to become the property of the British government? They bought the outpost for 58,291 dollars. Thus ended John Jacob Astor's association with the fur trade in the Pacific Northwest. His biographer, Kenneth Porter, remarked: "for all practical purposes, the careers of both the Pacific Fur Company and Astoria came to an end." Hiram M. Chittenden, who wrote much about the fur trade in the Pacific Northwest said: "there was not a could-have-been in the whole transaction that did not turn out adversely…"

Even the name Astoria was used no more. The British renamed the outpost Fort George. The abandonment of the fort in Astoria by the Americans left all the fur trade routes to the British. Keen competition developed between the Hudson's Bay Company and the North West Company. Indeed, so keen was the competition that agents of both companies resorted to ambush, arson, thievery, kidnapping and even murder to further the interests of their own company. Concern was raised as far away as London. Finally, in 1821, a merger was negotiated in London between the two great companies. The name Hudson's Bay Company was retained – no more North West Company.

With the merger came renewed interest in establishing secure fur routes, interspersed with trading posts all along the Oregon Trail, connecting with the trading posts already established across Canada, and culminating at the mouth of the Columbia, where ships would transport the goods to China. Haste was essential. Now that the war was over, Americans were showing renewed interest in a cross-country fur route.

Oregon history abounds with descriptions of the men who crossed this frontier. There was Dr. John McLaughlin, named by the Hudson's Bay Company as Chief Factor for the Columbia District. He had been a physician to the North West Company and is described as six feet four inches tall, with piercing eyes and a strong, raw-boned appearance. We have the following description by George Simpson, governor of the Northern Department and Columbia District, when they met by chance on the trail: "such a figure as I should not like to meet in a dark Night in one of the bye lanes in the neighborhood of London…He was dressed in Clothes that had once been fashionable, but now covered with a thousand patches of different Colors, his beard would do honor to the chin of a Grizzley Bear, his face and hands evidently Shewing up that he had not lost much time at his Toilette, loaded with Arms and his own herculean dimensions forming a tout ensemble that would convey a good idea of the highway men of former Days."

George Simpson himself was an interesting character. He had been born in Scotland, but employment in a London mercantile firm brought him to the attention of the Hudson's Bay Company. He was brilliant and climbed rapidly up the ladder of success. The official Hudson's Bay Company history says of him: "He had the imaginative vision of a Clive; he drew his plans on a scale that was continental" and "In him a clear orderly mind and a driving ambition were sustained by a physical vitality which carried him bouyantly through life." He was eventually knighted by the British government for his accomplishments.

After meeting on the trail to Oregon, Simpson and McLaughlin continued to Fort George (Astoria that was) together. They made preparations to completely redesign their Pacific Coast operations. They began by moving the headquarters post to a point on the north side of the Columbia River, opposite present-day Portland. They were certain that, no matter what, the territory north of the Columbia would always remain in British hands. They named their new post Fort Vancouver, after the great explorer.

By March 15, 1825, the new fort was complete and Simpson dedicated it. He recounted the day in his journal: "At Sun rise mustered all the people to hoist the Flag Staff of the new Establishment and in presence of the Gentlemen, Servants, Chiefs and Indians, I Baptised it by breaking a Bottle of Rum on the Flag Staff and repeating the following words in a loud voice, 'In behalf of the Hon. Hudson's Bay Company I hereby name this Establishment Fort Vancouver. God Save King George the Fourth' with three cheers … The object of nameing it after that distinguished navigator is to identify our claim to the Soil and Trade with his discovery of the River and Coast on behalf of Great Britain."

The Hudson's Bay Company's Fort Vancouver was to grow continually in importance. McLaughlin was in charge and he encouraged new trades, such as raising cattle and sheep, fishing and agriculture. They successfully grew corn, peas, oats, barley and wheat in the rich river soil. It became the leading port city where all goods from the inland were transported for shipment elsewhere and where supplies arrived. The fur trade grew in importance, along with Fort Vancouver's prosperity.

New settlers continued to arrive to swell Vancouver's population. Soon they established a carpenter shop, church, bake house, blacksmith shop, stables, a "hospital" and a flour mill. When the American, Lieutenant Charles Wilkes, visited Fort Vancouver in 1841, he wrote: "(It) is a large manufacturing, agricultural, and commercial depot, and there are few if any idlers, except the sick. Everybody seems to be in a hurry, whilst there appears to be no obvious reason for it."

Dr. McLaughlin remained in charge of Fort Vancouver for twenty-two years and was known for his tolerant but firm attitude toward the Indians, his business expertise and his warm hospitality to American settlers, traders and missionaries. He was deservedly known as the "Father of Oregon."

He established a vigorous export trade, especially in wheat and flour. By 1846, for example, he exported 6,000 barrels of flour to Alaska. He built a sawmill near Fort Vancouver and produced and sold lumber. He even exported some to Hawaii and he established a vigorous trade in salmon.

Fort Vancouver seems to have had a pleasant social life as well, holding balls, regattas and dinners for the entertainment of its citizens. They ate good food at polished tables set with silver and Spode, read good books and engaged in stimulating conversation. The wives of the officers were generally bright and intelligent half-castes.

As good as life was, the fact that the Hudson's Bay Company was a monopoly and without the benefit of competition was bound to be a source of dissatisfaction. They set their own prices for the sale of goods from London, usually with a 100 percent markup. And they set a firm price for the purchase of goods from the settlers – not subject to negotiation.

The Americans had not been idle in their efforts to obtain an influential position in Oregon since the War of 1812. Actually, Astoria was officially restored to the American government in the Convention of 1818, but nothing came of it. At the same time a treaty was signed between Great Britain and the United States granting joint occupation of the Oregon Territory for ten years. Oregon Territory now comprised an area that extended north to the 54°40' parallel and south to the 42nd; east to the Rocky Mountains and west to the Pacific Ocean. The Convention of 1818 also recognized the 49th parallel as the northern boundary of the United States as far west as the Rockies.

In 1823, Representative John Floyd of Virginia even had the foresight to introduce a bill in Congress that would recognize an American interest in Oregon country. He spoke of the importance of the Columbia River to American commerce. It would provide a safe harbor for whalers traveling from New England. It would also serve as a base for an established fur trade in the United States and it would provide a port in the

Pacific Northwest from which to carry on the China Trade. He also saw the territory as a place for eventual expansion. He could see settlers moving West to farm or open shops. But all this was too much for Congress to comprehend in 1823. They defeated the bill.

Subsequent negotiations between Great Britain and the United States eventually narrowed the controversy over boundary. The United States contended that its territory should extend west to the Pacific Ocean along the 49th parallel. Great Britain thought that the boundary should extend along the 49th parallel to the point where the Columbia River intersects it and then follow the line of the river south. Under this proposal, most of the current state of Washington would remain British. But great strides had been made to reduce the intransigence these positions.

Meanwhile, more and more settlers had been migrating to the Oregon Territory – almost all of them Americans. There were mountain men like Jedediah Smith, David Jackson and the Sublette brothers, William, Milton and Andrew, who set up trapping expeditions in the mountains and, as a sideline, sold supplies to other trappers, Indians and folks they ran into on the trail. Prices were high, but there was little choice. In 1826 scarlet cloth, for example, went for six dollars a yard; beaver traps for nine dollars and firewater for thirteen dollars and fifty cents a gallon. Outfitting became more profitable than trapping.

Hall Kelley was a Boston schoolteacher who had read Lewis and Clark's account of the West. In 1829 he formed a society dedicated to settling the West. He called it the American Society for Encouraging the Settlement of the Oregon Territory. In typical Puritan fashion, he felt that planned settlement would provide a refuge for the unfortunate, improve the moral character of the Indians and break Great Britain's hold on the West.

Kelley wrote many pamphlets and brochures promoting his enterprise and, although he had never been there himself, described the land in vivid phrases. "Much of the country within two hundred miles of the ocean, is favorable to cultivate," he said. "The valley of the Multnomah (Willamette) is extremely fertile...The Oregon is covered with heavy forests of timber...The production of vegetables, grain and cattle will require comparatively but little labor; these articles, together with the spontaneous growth of the soil, and the fruits of laborious industry, in general will find a market, at home, and thereby comfort and enrich the settlers. Surplus staple articles may be shipped from their doors to distant ports, and return a vast profit in trade."

Although Kelley's colonization efforts never materialized for him, his tracts stirred much interest. In fact, Nathaniel J. Wyeth thought it sounded as if the time was right to establish an American company that would rival the Hudson's Bay Company. Accordingly, he organized the Pacific Trading Company. He led an expedition to Oregon in 1832 that left St. Louis with twenty-four men. Sickness and disaster plagued them. They arrived at the gates of Fort Vancouver with only eleven. McLaughlin made it clear that he would not tolerate a competitive fur trading company but Wyeth had no money anyway. Several of his men elected to remain in Oregon but Wyeth went back to Boston. So much for an American rival to the Hudson's Bay Company.

Jason Lee, a minister for the Methodist Ministry Society, his nephew, Daniel Lee, also a minister, and their lay helpers Philip Edwards, Cyrus Shepard and Courtney M. Walker had joined the Wyeth expedition to set up a mission among the Indians. After spending some time at Fort Vancouver, they searched for a likely spot. Lee's choice was a lovely location in the Willamette Valley, ten miles north of the present site of Salem, Oregon. He wrote that it was "so situated as to form a central position from which missionary labors may be extended in almost every direction among the natives and those emigrants who may hereafter settle in that vast and fertile territory."

Lee immediately set about the task of building and organizing a school. A mere four years later he could boast to headquarters that he had admitted fifty-two Indian pupils to his school. His success so impressed the Mission Society that they sent thirteen more men and women in 1836.

Feeling the need for even more reinforcements, Lee traveled East in 1838. He must have been a great orator and enthusiastic about his topic, for this time the congregations supplied him with 100,000 dollars, thirty-two adults, eighteen children and a ship to bring them all West. They brought enough goods to set up a mission store, as well as tools to build even more homes, churches, schools and mission stations.

Chief among their new stations was the one at The Dalles. In 1841 Jason Lee reportedly baptized over 130 individuals and gave the sacraments to 500 at The Dalles. That does not necessarily mean, however, that all those Indians were converted to Christianity. Indeed, there is considerable evidence that the Methodist missionaries and the Indians understood very little about one another. During an eruption of Mt. St. Helens, for example, in 1843, the Indians exhibited terror of a God who would command fire to shoot into the air and cause the earth to shake. The missionaries exalted such a God and impulsively broke into song. The Indians were totally bewildered. Missionary theology dealt with ideas – Indian religion with things. It was hard to reconcile the two.

As the difficulty of the task of converting the Indians to Christianity became more apparent, interest in missionary work dwindled. The missionaries spent more and more of their time furthering the work of the settlement. They planted crops, increased their cattle herds and built even more houses, stables and stores. A visitor in 1841 noted, "As far as my personal observation went...they seem more occupied with the settlement of the country and in the agricultural pursuits than in the missionary labors."

Finally, in 1843, Lee was suspended from his post. He and his brother returned East. Nevertheless, many of the missionary band remained in the Willamette Valley as settlers. They eventually formed the nucleus that attracted so many future settlers to this lush land.

The coastal region and the Willamette Valley weren't the only places that attracted missionaries. In 1835 the American Board of Commissioners for Foreign Missions sent out Dr. Samuel Parker to see if they should set up missions in Oregon Territory. He was accompanied by young Dr. Marcus Whitman. They found lots of Indians to convert so, without even going the full distance to Fort Vancouver, Whitman returned East to bring out supplies and more assistants. He married his childhood sweetheart and brought her along. Reverend and Mrs. Henry Narman Spalding volunteered to come as well. These two women, except for Sacagawea, proved to be the first women to make the overland trip.

In order to carry even more supplies, they took wagons – later even converting one to a cart. Thus they were the first expedition to take a wagon as far as Fort Boise. It was only a matter of time before wagons would make the journey clear to the Pacific Ocean. Six months after arriving at Fort Vancouver, Narcissa Whitman gave birth to the first white child born west of the Continental Divide.

Dr. Parker had been busy while Dr. Whitman was in the

East. He had staked out a number of sites for his missions. He assigned the Whitmans to one on the Walla Walla River, about twenty miles from the Columbia. Dr. Parker noted, "A mission located on this fertile field would draw around it an interesting settlement, who would fix down to cultivate the soil and to be instructed. How easily might the plough go through these valleys, and what rich and abundant harvests might be gathered by the hand of industry."

And that's exactly what the Whitmans did. They planted fields of grain and corn and taught the Indians to do the same. The Nez Perce Indians were intelligent and industrious and they learned quickly. The Cayuse Indians were less so and kept their distance – even exhibiting hostility at times.

Catholic missionaries came too. In 1838 Father Francis N. Blanchet, of the Montreal diocese, arrived after an arduous journey of 5,325 miles from Montreal – a trip that had lasted six months. The Catholics set up missions on the Cowlitz River and near present-day Oregon City on the Willamette.

Cordial relations did not exist between the Catholics and the Protestants, to say the least. Had they ever? The British at Fort Vancouver and at other Hudson's Bay Company trading posts were mostly French-Canadian Catholics. They encouraged the Catholic priests. Competition between the two factions was keen. Father Blanchet extended his missions and was soon elevated to Bishop.

It was clear to most everyone by now that the fur trade was diminishing. Beaver, once been plentiful, was now scarce. Otters no longer abounded. Even McLaughlin, who still ran Fort Vancouver for the Hudson's Bay Company, wrote as early as 1836, "Every One Knows who is acquainted with the Fur trade that as the country becomes settled the Fur trade Must Diminish."

Several events took place that spurred a new interest in the settlement of the Oregon country. In 1836 the immensely popular novelist, Washington Irving, had written a two-volume work called *Astoria*. It was widely read. And that was only the beginning. Newspapers began to romanticize the West.

The cry was "Westward Ho!" By 1843 "Oregon Fever" had set in. That was the year of the Great Migration. It was the year that 875 new emigrants settled the Willamette Valley; the year that the first covered wagons made it as far as The Dalles and the year that 700 head of cattle were driven over the Oregon Trail.

In 1839 the population of the Willamette Valley was estimated at 100 souls. By 1843 the number had swollen to 1,500 – and all except sixty-one were American. Huge caravans now started the westward trek. By 1845, the population of the Territory had grown to 6,000.

It's hard for us to imagine today the rigors and hardships of cross-country travel by wagon train. It was imperative that strict discipline and time-schedules be maintained. The trains usually left St. Louis by mid-May, when the rivers had receded enough to ford and the grass was sufficient for the livestock. Our best accounts are from journals kept by the travelers themselves. Jesse Applegate came in the Great Migration of 1843. Later he wrote of his adventures:

"It is four o'clock a.m.; the sentinels on duty have discharged their rifles – the signal that the hours of sleep are over – and every wagon and tent is pouring forth its nights tenants, and slowly kindling smokes begin largely to rise and float away in the morning air...breakfast is to be eaten, the tents struck, the wagons loaded and the teams yoked and brought up in readiness to be attached to their respective wagons. All know when, at seven o'clock the signal to march sounds, that those not ready to take their proper places in the line of march must fall into the dusty rear for the day...

"The pilot, by measuring the ground and timing the speed of the horses, has determined the rate of each, so as to enable him to elect the nooning place as nearly as the requisite grass and water can be had at the end of five hours travel of the wagons...A corral is not formed at noon, but the wagons are drawn up in columns, four abreast, the leading wagon of each platoon on the left, the platoons being formed with that in view. This brings friends together at noon as well as at night.

"Today an extra session of the council is being held, to settle a dispute that does not admit of delay, between a proprietor and a young man who had undertaken to do a man's service on the journey for bed and board. Many such cases exist, and much interest is taken in the manner in which this high court, from which there is no appeal, will define the rights of each party in such engagements...

"It is now one o'clock; the bugle has sounded and the caravan has resumed its westward journey. It is in the same order – but the evening is far less animated than the morning march. A drowsiness has fallen apparently on man and beast...

"The sun is now getting low in the west, and at length the painstaking pilot is standing ready to conduct the train in the circle which he has previously measured and marked out, which is to form the invariable fortification for the night...Within ten minutes from the time the leading wagon halted, the barricade is formed, the teams unyoked and driven out to pasture. Everyone is busy preparing fires...to cook the evening meal, pitching tents and otherwise preparing for the night...The watches begin at eight o'clock p.m. and end at four o'clock a.m."

Credit for the Great Migration has often been given to Dr. Whitman but that is probably more myth than fact. It is true that in 1842 Whitman received a letter from the American Board advising him that it had decided to close his mission. Not **his** mission! He immediately returned East by horseback to argue his case. He traveled to New York, Washington and Boston, convincing all he spoke to that a practical route and safe passage to Oregon could be assured by continuation of the missions. It has been suggested that he also convinced folks of the need to save Oregon from the British.

Whitman even had an interview with that famous newspaperman, Horace Greeley, editor of the *New York Tribune*, but he didn't convince this doubting Thomas. Greeley would later pen the statement that has been paraphrased as "Go West, Young Man, Go West," but in 1843 he wrote: "This emigration of more than 1,000 persons in one body to Oregon wears an aspect of insanity. For what do they brave the desert, the wilderness, the savage, the snowy precipices of the Rocky Mountains, the weary summer march, the storm drenched bivouac and the gnawings of famine?" When he said "Go West" he meant Chicago, perhaps St. Louis or even Ohio, but never Oregon – that was insanity!

Be that as it may, with this new influx of emigrants from the United States there was more and more dissatisfaction with British rule. In 1843 some of the Americans in the Willamette Valley got together to draw up a provisional constitution – much as their ancestors had done less than 100 years earlier in Philadelphia. They included a bill of rights with provisions requiring fairness to Indians and prohibiting slavery. It even included an innovative new method for filing land claims.

The cry for independence from Britain was joined by the rest of the nation, especially those in the Mississippi Valley. The United States was officially still offering to settle at the 49th parallel but the nation wanted the territory north to the 54°40' parallel. The cry of "54-40 or fight!" was chanted in legislatures and in the streets.

So intense was the nation's desire to annex Oregon that

they elected a president in 1844 who was committed to the cause, James Knox Polk. This President knew what he wanted: tariff reductions, California, treasury reform and settlement of the Oregon boundary question. He intended to be a one-term president, so he was in a hurry. In his inaugural address he boldly claimed all the Oregon Territory north to 54°40'. To prove how reasonable he was, though, he offered to settle with Britain at the 49th a few days later. Britain refused. Polk publicly went back to the 54°40' position and proclaimed that the United States would accept nothing less.

Loud protestations on both sides continued through all of 1845. But when, in 1846, the British offered to settle at 49 at least as far as the Puget Sound and then mid-channel through the Strait of Juan de Fuca to the Pacific, Polk demurred. He refused to commit himself, but deferred to the Senate for "advice and consent." They quickly gave it and the treaty was signed on June 15, 1846.

It was characteristic of the great John McLaughlin, still Chief Factor of the Hudson's Bay Company, that he was one of the first to sign the oath of loyalty to the new provincial government. Throughout the years he had remained kind to the Indians, welcomed American settlers, often providing them with money and food from his own storehouse, and caring for their sick himself.

How was he rewarded? The British attacked him as a traitor. He wrote: "why? Because I acted as a Christian, saved American citizens, men, women and children from the Indian tomahawk and enabled them to take farms to support their families...?"

The Americans distrusted McLaughlin. He was British and Catholic. They eventually confiscated all his property. Ten years later, as an old and sick man, he wrote a plea to a young Oregon politician: "I might better have been shot forty years ago than to have lived here and tried to build up a family and an estate in this government. I became a citizen of the United States in good faith. I planted all I had here, and the government confiscated my property. Now what I want to ask of you is that you will give your influence after I am dead to have this property go to my children. I have earned it as other settlers have earned theirs, and it ought to be mine and my heirs'." His lands were eventually restored to his heirs but the "Father of Oregon" died penniless and disillusioned in 1857.

Things were not all that rosy for the Whitmans near Walla Walla either. Wagon trains made their mission a regular stop on the way West but when the emigrant train of 1847 arrived, many of the children were sick with the measles. Soon the disease spread to the Indians, who had no built-up immunity to the disease. The white children recovered but the Indians died. The Indians took this as a sign that Dr. Whitman was giving special attention to the whites and not enough to them. They wondered if maybe he was even giving them poison.

On October 29, 1847, the Cayuse Indians swooped down on the hapless mission. They scalped and slaughtered Dr. Whitman, Narcissa and many others unlucky enough to be present. Of the seventy-two people in the mission, the Indians killed fourteen and they took many hostages.

The Whitman Massacre raised strong feelings that Congress should declare the Oregon country a territory of the United States. They sent a message to Washington, "Our relations with the proud and powerful tribes of Indians residing east of the Cascade Mountains, hitherto uniformly amicable and pacific, have recently assumed quite a different character. They have shouted the war whoop and crimsoned their tomahawks in the blood of our citizens...To repel the attacks of so formidable a foe, and protect our families and property from violence and rapine, will require more strength than we possess...we have a right to expect your aid, and you are in justice bound to extend it..."

Finally, in 1848, Congress created territorial status for the old Oregon country. President Polk lost no time in appointing General Joseph Lane the first Territorial Governor of Oregon. Mountain man Joe Meek, who had sped to Washington with the terrible news of the Whitman Massacre and the subsequent Cayuse Wars, was appropriately named U.S. Marshal to the new Territory.

Lane and Meek lost no time in heading west. Because of the approach of winter they took the Southern route, arriving in San Francisco just as the California Gold Rush fever struck. They sailed by ship to the Columbia River, by canoe up the Columbia and finally up the Willamette River to Oregon City, site of the first territorial government. Ironically, news that Congress had created the Oregon Territory reached the outpost via the Hawaiian Islands, nearly a month before Lane himself.

Oregon City was quite the metropolis by then. Its location on the Willamette Falls made it ideal for harnessing energy to power mills. It boasted the first newspaper, the *Oregon Spectator*, a population of 500, two blacksmiths, four tailors, two churches, two saloons, two hatters, two silversmiths, a tannery, two sawmills, two grist mills, a cooper, a cabinet maker and about seventy-five houses. In fact, the town had been founded by Dr. John McLaughlin when he retired from the Hudson's Bay Company in 1846. It was his land in Oregon City and ownership of the Imperial Mills which he founded, that were later confiscated by the new government.

There was plenty for a new governor to do, that's for sure. To begin with, those Cayuse Indians continued to be very troublesome. The massacre of the Whitmans was only the beginning. Although some Cayuse had attempted to surrender, return the captives, apologize for the massacre and call the whole thing off, others were more belligerent. Oregon residents felt strongly that the murderers should be apprehended and punished. Sporadic fighting occurred throughout 1848.

On Governor Lane's arrival, preparations were immediately made for a fresh attack. The Cayuse recognized these reinforcements as formidable. They offered to negotiate again. They would surrender the murderers in exchange for peace. Lane agreed. The five Indian warriors were handed over to federal officers in The Dalles. They were taken to Oregon City, tried, convicted of murder and hanged in 1850. Three years of Indian wars were finally over. Governor Lane's swift and decisive treatment of the Cayuse Indians set the tone for settling future disagreements with the Indians and was the example followed by subsequent governors.

Meanwhile, back in Washington, D.C., Polk had been replaced as president by Zachary Taylor. As usual, a new administration means new heads for administrative posts. Taylor first offered the post of governor of Oregon Territory to an unknown young Whig party worker from Illinois by the name of Abraham Lincoln. He declined the honor, so the second governor was General John P. Gaines. Governor Lane continued to promote the interests of Oregon, however, by being elected as Oregon's delegate to Congress. In this capacity, he worked hard for passage of an suitable land bill.

For Oregon settlers, the Donation Land Law, passed by Congress in September, 1850, was perhaps the answer to a dream. It assured those who endured the hardships of the overland trek of a place of their own. Principally, it had four tenets: (1) A survey would be made of all land in Oregon. (2) Every white or half-breed male over eighteen years of age, who had occupied and cultivated his land for four years prior to

December 1850, who was already a Territorial citizen or would declare allegiance before December 1851, would receive 320 acres of land. If married, husband and wife each would be entitled to 320 acres. (3) Any white male citizen at least twenty-one years of age, arriving between December 1850 and December 1855 would receive 160 acres. Double if married. (4) Heirs to claimants would be recognized under law. The law was later amended to allow an outright purchase of the land for one dollar and twenty-five cents an acre if the prospective buyer had been in residence on the land for two years – in case he didn't want to wait the full four years to get it free. In 1855 the donation law expired.

What a rush up the wedding aisle those laws created! Women were as scarce in Oregon as in other territorial communities. Nevertheless, wedding bells rang incessantly. Young girls barely beyond adolescence became brides, as did Indian maidens. Fully half of the land claims were from married men.

In those few intervening years, the law encouraged a tremendous migration to the West. In 1845, the population of the territory was 6,000; by 1849 the number had grown to 9,083 (8,785 were United States citizens, the rest Canadians); by 1850 the total had risen to 13,294. Between 1850 and 1855, between 30,000 and 35,000 new settlers arrived.

Agriculture was the primary occupation and small communities throughout Oregon flourished. Even the little town of Portland, founded in 1850, boasted a population of 2,874 by 1860.

"There's gold in California!" The word buzzed through Oregon Territory. What an impact it had. California gold channeled at least one half of the able bodied men – formerly farmers – off to a new interest. But, on the other hand, the established trading posts prospered as a new market for goods in California increased. Portland, especially, profited. More and more ships, and of ever greater size, collected meat, flour, eggs and lumber for the mining camps to the south.

The Hudson's Bay Company had moved its headquarters to Fort Victoria, on the southern tip of Vancouver Island, some time earlier. Even so, it retained possession of Fort Vancouver and was granted "free and open" navigation of the Columbia River as part of the Treaty of 1846. Because of the British interests, former Hudson's Bay Company territories on the lower Columbia River were not opened to settlers until 1859.

Even the area around the Puget Sound was still virtually unsettled in 1845. It appears that the first settlers north of the Columbia River were Michael T. Simmons and his eight companions from Kentucky. They chose a site at the southern tip of Puget Sound and called it New Market, later changing it to Tumwater. Mike promptly set up the first saw mill and did very well indeed, thank you! Four years later, in 1849, he sold it to Bing Crosby's ancestor, Clanrick Crosby, for the splendid sum of 35,000 dollars (Bing's great-grandfather had just built a magnificent house in Portland). Mike Simmons was a rich man. Soon he owned the first merchant ship to ship goods regularly to and from the Puget Sound, and he opened the first American post office and store. Where? In the fledgling village of Olympia.

Even so, there was certainly no great rush north. In 1849 there were still merely 304 inhabitants north of the Columbia River, and most of those were employees of the Hudson's Bay Company. But by 1850, the numbers had reached 1,049 and, by 1853, a whopping 4,000. It was understandable that growth was slow. Much of the choice land was still controlled by the Hudson's Bay Company. Also, men with families were under strong pressure to settle where the relative conveniences of houses with roofs and floors, stores to buy goods, schools for children and hospitals for the sick made life almost civilized.

Indeed, when settlements did begin to spring up around the Puget Sound, they were virtually isolated from the settlers of Oregon. Communication took place either by overland route – mostly horseback or mule – or by boat.

That may be one reason why it took so long to settle the Puget Sound. When folks did come, though, it was like an explosion. In 1851 the Arthur Denny family traveled overland from Cherry Grove, Illinois. Denny had married Mary Ann Boren and she accompanied him on the trip. On arriving in Portland, they were disappointed to find a thriving town. Clearly what they wanted was virgin territory. They heard about the prospects for a new settlement in the Puget Sound and, after taking a look for themselves, gathered up their possessions and set out.

They boarded the schooner *Exact* and eight days later landed on an isolated stretch of beach, previously staked out for them by David Denny (Arthur's brother), John Low and Lee Terry. In all there were twenty-four people, all set to establish a new community on these bleak shores.

What they found sounds positively miserable. A passenger on the *Exact* described pulling away from port and seeing the boxes with all the party's earthly belongings sitting on the beach in the driving rain as the incoming tide lapped at them. She also described the scene of the women and children crying so hard (or was it the rain?) that their bonnets drooped in their eyes and remained plastered to their cheeks.

It's hard to imagine, but the men must have felt much better about their situation. Indeed, Denny says, "Our first work was to provide shelter for the winter, and we finished the house begun by my brother and Low. We all took shelter in it from the rain, which was falling more or less every day, but we did not regard it with much concern and seldom lost any time on that account."

Optimism, and maybe even enthusiasm for their new location, must have had much to do with its christening too. They knew a metropolis would eventually rise on these shores. The Terry brothers were from New York and everyone knew that New York was the greatest city anywhere. Why not name their western province after their old home? And so it was. They named this barren beach New York. It was later lengthened to New York Alki – New York bye and bye.

As advantageous as this new site was, it didn't quite suit Denny. That's when he started looking around. He, Boren and Bell finally settled on a place across the bay, where a deep harbor promised to dock ships someday; where the forests extended right down to the harbor and where flat pasture land was abundant.

The Donation Land Law had brought them there. On February 15, 1852, Arthur Denny, Carson Boren and William Bell filed their claim on land that would later become Seattle. Charles Terry and John Low preferred the New York site and they filed their claim for it.

One of the most beloved characters in Pacific Northwest history, or perhaps any history, was the man who showed up on Denny's doorstep only a few months after the folks settled into their places in Seattle. Doc Maynard was a character – no doubt about it. But until his departure from Cleveland, Ohio, he had led a respectable but miserable existence.

It seems that he did all of the things that were expected of him. He graduated from medical school, set up a profitable practice, married, had two children, joined the Masonic Lodge and became a leading citizen. He knew things weren't great at home, but coming from a staunch Puritan family (he was of solid Vermont stock) he accepted that as his lot.

Until 1841 that is. One night, as he testified later: "in the month of April of the year last aforesaid (1841) on returning home from visiting a patient at about the hour of ten o'clock in the night – found my wife lying with a certain John Hemrick in an obscene manner. That the undersigned had previously doubted her chastity but had never before seen anything positively confirming his suspicions." Actually, it seems that most of the able-bodied men in Cleveland were intimately acquainted with Lydia Maynard.

He didn't leave her right away; the children were only eleven and seven years old, and he didn't feel he could properly provide for them and his wife yet. He stayed around for another nine years until finally one day when he had had enough. Her extracurricular activities had diminished not a bit since the great discovery – in fact she seemed to enjoy flaunting her amorous affairs. All of Cleveland knew.

He left her the house, two children who could then take care of themselves, and sufficient money to sustain her for the rest of her life, as long as she was prudent in her investments. Divorce didn't occur to him.

He figured they'd certainly need doctors in the new land opening up out West, and tentatively decided to go to California. In April, 1850, Doc Maynard made his way from Cleveland to St. Joseph, Missouri, where he easily attached himself to a prosperous wagon train headed for the gold-rich country of California. He was forty-two years old, an advanced age in those days to make such a journey.

As usual, the trip was not an easy one, but Doc Maynard didn't have any particular hardships either. Until the cholera epidemic hit, that is. Fresh from treating cholera in Cleveland most of 1849, Doc Maynard was as used to it as the common cold. He knew that the use of calomel worked best. He also kept his patients warm and comfortable, boiled all water and gave them liberal doses of opium. He knew the opium would relax them and, if they were going to die anyway, the opium would make their passage to the next world infinitely easier. Doc Maynard knew what to do.

Not so with many doctors. The World Health Organization, commenting on the treatment of cholera in the United States in 1850, said: "your chances of surviving an attack were about as good as though you had been shot in the stomach at point-blank range...maybe fifty percent. On the other hand, if you fell into the hands of the average doctor, your chances of dying rose to about ninety percent."

That was especially true on the trail it seems. One man wrote: "Cholera waited in the brackish streams and waterholes, left by one party, to be passed on to the next group following across the plains. The route westward was marked with wooden crosses and stone cairns, the crosses often bearing only a word, and that was cholera. Nowhere could the disease have been more terrifying than on those trails, where men died without physicians, without ministers and without friends."

But the story of Doc Maynard is a love story. Remember Mike Simmons, the most prosperous man in the Puget Sound country? Also the postmaster and first store owner from Olympia? Seems he had a mother and two sisters, Catherine and Susanna, and the sisters had husbands. They had all fallen on tough times in Pike country, Illinois, so Mike persuaded them to join him out West. They left Missouri in March 1851, but along the way the mother, Catherine's husband, Israel Broshears, and Catherine, as well as at least half the rest of their party, were stricken with cholera. Broshears, Mrs. Morton and six others in the party died. Then, as if by magic, entered Doc Maynard. He wasn't riding on a white horse, nor was he in shining armor. In fact, he was on a mule wearing dirty trail clothes. No matter. He ministered to the sick and buried the dead. And he comforted the bereaved widow, Catherine.

Driving a wagon was no job for a woman and, in Doc's words, he "made arrangements to shift my duds to the widows wagon..." The Doc really knew nothing about driving a wagon either, but he soon learned. His kindness to the other members of their party and to animals soon touched Catherine's heart. On the long journey to the Puget Sound the doctor and Catherine fell in love. So much for Doc's trip to California.

However, scandal touched the party when Susanna and her husband refused to travel with Maynard and Catherine any longer. It seems that Susanna was jealous. That left these two unmarried folk to travel alone together for over sixty days. In 1851 that just wasn't done. It damaged the woman's reputation irreparably. But they really had no choice.

On arriving in Olympia, Maynard and Catherine headed straight for Mike Simmons' place. They told him the story and Doc professed his love for and desire to marry Catherine – just as soon as the problem with his extant wife was settled.

Meantime, Catherine moved in with Mike and his family, and Doc started cutting wood nearby to be close to Catherine. Eventually Doc took his huge stack of wood to San Francisco and sold it for 16,000 dollars, making him a man of property again. But Catherine's family didn't like her romance with Maynard at all.

Catherine's family was as proper as any proper Bostonian family might be, and they looked with extreme disfavor on her alliance with Maynard. Thomas Prosch, Maynard's principal biographer says: "Mrs. Broshears (Catherine) soon found herself to be in high favor with the bachelors and widowers, and she was evidently regarded by them as a catch of the best character. Her people speedily saw the direction of things, and they tried to direct it into quarters to suit themselves and their own ideas of propriety and desirability..."

"Knowing that Dr. Maynard was a married man, from his own admission, they disapproved the bent and inclination shown by him and their widowed sister. They made suggestions of other men, introduced them, and did what they could to break up the alliance between Maynard and Mrs. Broshears. They restrained her somewhat of her liberty and prevented her from going with him when they could."

Mike Simmons finally forced Doc Maynard out of town. But Doc was clever. To get a divorce was difficult, if not impossible, unless several witnesses would testify that they had seen the accused perform an act of adultery. Then there had to be a messy trial. Although Maynard had letters attesting to his wife's infidelity, her family was prominent in Cleveland and nobody would openly testify against her. The only other recourse was to have a divorce granted directly by the legislature, and that wasn't much better. Since the legislature was a public body, all business before it was public knowledge and widely reported by the newspapers. Doc would do anything to protect Catherine from humiliation and further loss of reputation.

It was now 1852 and Doc Maynard had moved on to Seattle. He was active in local politics and had drafted a bill asking that the territory north of the Columbia River be allowed to become an independent territory with its own government. When he filed the bill in Salem, Oregon, he slipped a little bill of divorce in with it. The latter was granted in December of 1852. On January 15, 1853, there was a new Mrs. Maynard.

By all accounts the marriage was a happy one in all respects. Doc and Catherine shared in the growth of Seattle for twenty years, until he died in 1873.

One interesting and bewildering postscript should be mentioned, though. As Doc's wealth increased, word of it reached Lydia back in Cleveland. Maynard had obtained his land as part of the Donation Land Law. An unscrupulous lawyer showed up on Lydia's doorstep claiming that he had found a flaw that, if she gave him 500 dollars, would entitle her to one half of Doc's property. She gave him the 500 dollars and then showed up on Doc's doorstep herself. Not only that, but she moved in with Doc and Catherine while she testified against them and tried to deprive them of their property. Doc and Catherine won the battle. It seems impossible to imagine that either of them would tolerate Lydia in their household while she fought them, but there you have it: truth is often more improbable than fiction.

Doc was a character – no doubt about it. Word has it that one day during Lydia's sojourn (probably after imbibing too much, as he had occasion to do) he called the newspaper and invited them out to take a photograph of a man walking down Main Street with a wife on each arm. They came and, sure enough, along came Doc with his two ladies.

However, there's much more to Doc Maynard's contribution to Pacific Northwest history than romantic folklore. When he showed up on Denny's doorstep he did so with Chief Sealth in tow, and he had an idea about setting up a salmon-packing plant. It was a good idea and Denny immediately saw the value of it. A business would bring prosperity to their enterprise. He offered Doc a grant of land, which Doc accepted. In fact, the other claimants all obligingly shifted their claims northeast to give Maynard a nice piece of waterfront.

They did the same for Henry Yesler when he arrived in October of 1852. He wanted to build a steam sawmill. It seems he had all the equipment stored in Portland already. Boren and Maynard agreed to shift their claims again to make room for Yesler on the waterfront.

All this shifting resulted in a passel of confusion before long. Denny and Boren filed their plan for the city streets one morning, while Maynard – a bit hung over from a joyous celebration the night before – filed his plan that afternoon. On Doc's land, the streets ran almost north-south, but on the rest they went off in a more east-west fashion. Yesler's mill was right in between. All that confusion never has been fully straightened out. The city just bends where the two sections meet.

All the towns up and down the Washington Territory vied for Yesler's mill. Doc and Denny felt fortunate indeed when he chose their town as his site. Yesler never was able to make that mill turn a profit, but the plume of smoke rising above it was a magnet for new settlers entering the bay. If it had a mill, they reasoned, it must be a profitable town.

We can thank Yesler and his sawmill for a phrase familiar to our present-day language. Yesler would cut his logs up on the hill just above his mill. Then he'd slide them down the hill to the mill. The track of dirt became rutted and distinct. Everyone called it "Skid Road". The name stuck, and its use spread to other towns as well. It was only later that the term became slang for "the downward path to ruin or poverty". Now, many towns have an area known locally as "Skid Row". That, according to the dictionary, means "a run-down urban area frequented by vagrants."

Now that they had a mill and a salmon-packing business, they had a real town. What would they call it? Surely, nothing would match New York Alki for grandness. When they received their land plan back from the recording office, someone had written "Duwamps" on it. Was Doc ever upset! That would never do for the name of a fine city! Chief Sealth had proven a firm friend of the new settlers, especially of Doc Maynard. Why not name the city after him? No one objected at all, except that they agreed on an anglicized version, calling it Seattle. Only

Chief Sealth was worried. Indian legend has it that whenever a dead man's name is mentioned, he turns over in his grave. Sealth wanted to rest in peace. Nevertheless, he agreed and lived to become proud of the honor.

Meanwhile, back in the rest of the territory, things were progressing nicely. Oregon wanted statehood. But leaders in Salem and the Willamette Valley considered that to govern an area that extended as far as the 49th parallel was a big task indeed. Nearly everyone agreed that the land north to the Columbia River and south to the 42nd parallel was plenty. So, when those cheeky folk north of the Columbia asked for territorial status of their own, the Oregon legislature agreed. They sent a joint resolution to Washington, D.C., and on March 2, 1853, the separate territory of Washington was created. President Franklin Pierce named Major Isaac Ingall Stevens as first territorial governor. In gratitude, residents named one of the largest counties after Pierce. They named the county where Seattle is located after Pierce's Vice President, William King.

Washingtonians were delighted with their Territorial status. *The Columbian*, Olympia's newspaper, said, "No longer in the hands of go-betweens, we have become 'a people' within ourselves. Progress is our watchword. Our destiny is in the keeping of God, the National Government, and our own judgment."

Meanwhile, relations with the Indians were still not great. The Indians had seen their resources being depleted. Several demanded that the white man leave. They were "frightening the fish away from the streams. Already there are fewer elk and deer in the forests, fewer ducks and geese in the marshes, fewer berries in the woods, because of white man's presence." They said, "This is my country; I was in it when those large trees were very small. My heart is sick with fighting, but I want to live in my country."

The summer of 1855 was the year of the Indian treaties and they were conducted by Governor Stevens. At the conclusion of the Walla Walla Council, all of the major tribes in Washington Territory had ceded their lands to the United States. In return, they were granted small "reservations" where they would maintain absolute control and would be granted cash payments. In the case of the Yakima Indians, for example, as much as 200,000 dollars – to be paid over a twenty-year period.

Yet, for all the white man's promises, no money came. The Indians watched white men build cabins, raise livestock, plant crops and fence in their land, while the Indians had less and less to live on. They lost confidence in the white man and became convinced that the promises would never be kept.

The summer of treaties was followed by three years of war, not all of it with the Indians. The war between Governor Stevens and Chief Justice Lander was typical. At the first outbreak of conflict, Governor Stevens declared martial law. "How dare he!" was the reaction of Chief Justice Lander. Lander had been out fighting the Indians, but he returned immediately and opened up his court for business. Not only that, but he ordered Governor Stevens arrested for contempt. So, what do you think happened next? Stevens had Lander arrested for desertion of his military duties. They resolved this dilemma in a unique way. Stevens released Lander from jail. Lander imposed a fine on Stevens and Stevens pardoned himself. So much for frontier justice!

But not so much for the Indian Wars. They continued through 1858, when all of the Indians finally surrendered. The price was high in lives, livestock and farmland. Fields had gone untended for three years. Especially in Washington Territory, where the toll was highest, new manpower was deflected elsewhere and the resentment and distrust between white man and Indian continued.

Somehow, the folks in Seattle escaped most of this unpleasantness. Oh, there were wars alright, but Chief Sealth never lost confidence in his white friends. In 1854, when Governor Stevens called the coastal tribes together on Elliott Bay to negotiate the treaties, Chief Sealth had prepared a speech that is unique in its prophecy and naiveté. It's a long speech. Here is but a small piece:

"The Great – and I presume – good White Chief sends us word that he wants to buy our lands but is willing to allow us to reserve enough to live on comfortably. This indeed appears generous, for the Red Man no longer has rights that he need respect, and the offer may be wise also, for we are no longer in need of a vast country...

"Our dead will never forget this beautiful world that gave them being. They still love its winding rivers, its great mountains and its sequestered vales, and they ever yearn in tenderest affection over the lonely-hearted living, and often return to visit, guide and comfort them...

"And when the last Red Man shall have perished from the earth and his memory among the White men shall have become a myth, these shores will swarm with the invisible dead of my tribes; and when your children's children shall think themselves alone in the fields, the store, the shop, upon the highway or in the silence of the pathless woods, they will not be alone. In all the earth there is no place dedicated to your solitude.

"The White man will never be alone. Let him be just and deal kindly with my people, for the dead are not powerless. Dead – did I say? There is no death. Only a change of worlds."

The Indian Wars didn't hinder growth in the region one bit, though. By 1860 the population of Washington Territory alone had grown to 11,594 and by 1870 to 23,995.

That was small compared to Oregon. Records show that Oregon had 60,000 inhabitants in its rich farming valleys and towns by 1857. They were, indeed, becoming quite sophisticated. In that year alone, they shipped 60,000 barrels of flour, 3,000,000 pounds of bacon and pork, 250,000 pounds of butter, 25,000 bushels of apples, 40,000 dollars-worth of chickens and eggs, 200,000 dollars-worth of lumber, 75,000 dollars-worth of fruit trees and 52,000 head of cattle. The total value of all these exports amounted to 3,200,000 dollars. Not bad for a territory that hadn't even been granted statehood.

Now that Washington had territorial status and the Indian problems were solved, Oregonians did feel it was time to push for statehood. The biggest question in Congress was whether to admit Oregon as a "slave" or "non-slave" state. No one in tough Oregon territory had slaves, that's for sure, but Congress was trying its best to maintain an absolute balance. Until a new "slave" state could be admitted, there was no hope for Oregon. Nevertheless, in November 1857, 10,000 Oregon voters approved a measure for statehood and against slavery. Finally, in 1859, Congress approved the statehood bill and President Buchanan signed it into law. Oregon became the 33rd state. When Oregon was admitted as a state, Washington Territory was enlarged to include a portion of Wyoming, all of Idaho and parts of Montana.

Less than a year after Oregon's admission, a new president, Abraham Lincoln, was elected and the issue of slavery erupted. As far away as they were from the Civil War, Oregonians were not spared its effects. They sent men to the battlefields. Major Stevens was promoted to Brigadier General. He died in 1862 while leading his troops in the Battle of Chantilly.

"There was gold in them hills in Canada!" With this discovery came hordes of miners who needed to buy provisions and clothing and who, after their big "strike," needed a little fun and entertainment. Portland and Seattle became the stopping-off place of boats on their way to Victoria and the mine fields along the Fraser River. In 1866 alone, it was reported that over 500,000 dollars-worth of goods were taken across the United States/Canada border.

Portland and Seattle became the provision points for miners bound for the gold fields in Montana, too. After all, Western Montana was still part of Washington Territory, but it was a long way from Portland.

Soon there was talk of creating a new Idaho Territory. Sure enough, in 1863 they did just that! This left the present state of Washington as a separate territory. The new Idaho Territory included Western Montana and part of Wyoming – a vast area.

Mining was for the restless. It attracted a migrant population who, virtually overnight, would turn a sleepy town of fifty into a roaring mass of 5,000 boisterous men. Adventurers all, they were the ones not willing to make their fortune by patiently tilling the soil – no matter how much land might be given to them by the government. Get rich quick was their scheme. No idlers either, these folk! They believed in working hard and then in playing hard. Coming back into town after a week or two in the mine fields, they expected to find lots of saloons, lots of women and lots of tolerance among the settlers. They were just as likely to move on as quickly as they arrived, leaving a ghost town behind.

Communication between Pacific Northwest towns had always been difficult. No roads existed until the mid-nineteenth century. But once they did, stagecoaches weren't far behind. Used throughout the East for over 100 years, they were a welcome sight to isolated Westerners. By the 1850s regular stage coach service was established from Oregon City and Corvallis, "rain or no rain – mud or no mud – load or no load – but not without pay."

Finally, by 1860, stage service was opened between Portland, Oregon, and Sacramento, California – and on a regular basis too. A stage left both Portland and Sacramento every morning at 6.00 a.m., sweeping through over sixty regular stops along the way. They carried mail and passengers, assuring the arrival of both in the speedy time of seven days.

By 1868, there was even an East to West route traveling across country in the amazing time of twenty-four days, eighteen hours and thirty-five minutes. This astounding feat was accomplished by John Butterfield and William Fargo. Because of their enterprise, they were awarded the Post Office contract for a fee of 600,000 dollars annually. On the completion of the first journey of 2,700 miles from St. Louis to San Francisco, President Buchanan wrote to John Butterfield: "I cordially congratulate you upon the result. It is a glorious triumph for civilization and the Union."

It wasn't long after that that folks asked, as a special favor and for extra remuneration, that packages be carried as well. When the package was especially valuable, it was worthwhile to the owner to pay a special agent just to bring it. Soon "express" companies were springing up all over the place. They would carry gold dust from the mining town to the assay office; jewelry from a bank on the East Coast to a young girl on her wedding day in San Francisco, and stock certificates from one bank to another.

Henry Wells joined with William Fargo and they started an express operation on the Atlantic seaboard, but they quickly expanded to the West Coast. They moved their company headquarters to San Francisco and were soon the largest "express" company around. By 1860, they had 147 express offices up and down the coast and boasted a profit of 151,200 dollars. When Wells and Fargo bought out the Holladay

Overland Mail and Express Company, with its route from Atchison on the Missouri River to The Dalles on the Columbia, they gained a virtual monopoly in the stagecoach and express business. The name Wells Fargo was esteemed, even venerated. Everyone knew they'd get the job done.

Stagecoach drivers were a colorful lot. They were variously called "knights of the lash" or "whips." The best wagons were the Concord coaches, and they were the ones most often employed by Wells Fargo. They were strong and dependable. Because of their design they might even have been comfortable. With braces and leather straps, the passenger compartment actually rolled, rather than bouncing and jerking when the coach hit one of the numerous holes and ruts in the road. It could accommodate lots of passengers and baggage too. Nine persons would sit inside, two alongside the driver and up to twelve more on the top. It was said that: "Time was...when the man who held the ribbons over a six-horse team on the summits of the Sierra and in the canyons of the Coast and Cascade ranges was more highly esteemed than the millionaire or the statesman who rode behind him."

Everyone knew about the best. They were as famous as latter-day movie stars. There was Charlie McConnell, for instance. A rider said of him: "He handled his horses and worked the heavy brake and smoked cigars and chatted unceasingly to his two boxseat passengers, doing all equally well." No small feat.

Let it never be said, however, that travel by stagecoach was pleasant and enjoyable. There was never enough leg room; if you were relegated to a position on top, you had to hang on for dear life to avoid being toppled off as you passed over ruts and around corners ("no dozing up there, please!"); inside, your head was always hitting something and you emerged at your destination covered with dust or mud.

New England was so civilized by comparison. They had long ago built cozy taverns and inns along the way to allow the traveler comfort when taking a bite to eat and drink, and a warm, comfortable bed to sleep in at night. Not so in the Pacific Northwest. Even makeshift farmhouse inns, where an enterprising housewife felt she could earn a bit of extra money, were crude and mean and at great distances from one another. When a hungry, tired traveler sought food, it was barely palatable. One brave soul described it: "(We were) fed chiefly on small, square bits of tough, fried meat, with fried potatoes and, sometimes, pie. (This last you would eat of more freely were it not for the legions of houseflies, which dispute with you every mouthful!)"

Stagecoach travel in Washington Territory was secondary to waterway travel for many years. A traveler going from Portland to Seattle would travel down the Willamette River, then down the Columbia to the Cowlitz River and up that a ways before transferring to canoe and then finally to a stage to cover rough roads filled with several feet of mud, winding through dense forests.

A traveler in 1866 wrote to Horace Greeley of the *New York Tribune*: "I'm in great luck sure, for I'm here alive... And if human nature ever gets into a condition to appreciate and properly value a soft clean bed, or a clean cloth bountifully spread with everything good, it is at this end of the stage line from Olympia... At every step of his progress the question arises, how is relief of this intolerable suffering to be obtained...The great want of the Territory is the want of roads and the road of all other roads most needed is this from Olympia to the Columbia River..."

Actually, to the men of Seattle, the lack of roads was the least of their problems. They longed for women! True, they could take up with Indian women, but that left something to be desired. Bow legs, obesity and flattened skulls were not considered personal attractions, even in Seattle, at that time. Even their luxuriant black tresses were obtained at a price. Seems they washed their hair frequently in urine and then gave it a good conditioner of fish oil.

Charles Prosch, editor of the *Puget Sound Herald,* had an idea. He ran an advertisement: "Attention, Bachelors: Believing that our only chance of a realization of the benefits and early attainment of matrimonial alliances depends upon the arrival in our midst of a number of the fair sex from the Atlantic States, and that, to bring about such an arrival a united effort and action are called for on our part, we respectfully request a full attendance of all eligible and sincerely desirous bachelors in this community to assemble on Tuesday evening next in Delin and Shorey's building to devise ways and means to secure this much needed and desirable emigration to our shores." It was only too true. The proportion of men to women was about ten to one. Lots of men showed up, but other than printing the advertisement in Eastern newspapers, they could figure no way of getting women there. Not only did Prosch offer marriage to eligible ladies, but he let it be known that there was also a need for dressmakers, cooks, schoolteachers and laundresses.

Into the breach stepped Asa Mercer. He took the town by storm. To start with, he had built the area's first university building, becoming its first president and sole faculty member. It was a grand affair – a white-columned building with a domed cupola, high on a hill just above the town. Everyone was most impressed with this first Territorial University.

Next, Mercer decided to take on the woman problem. He reasoned that the Civil War had probably killed off lots of the male population in the East so there'd be plenty of eligible young girls around, eager to come to Washington. If he could raise enough money, he could ship willing New England women out to Seattle by the hundreds – maybe, he speculated, in lots of 500. But he couldn't raise the money. Maybe they thought he was a crackpot. He could, in fact, only raise enough money for his one-way passage to the East. Undaunted, he went anyway.

Up and down New England he traveled, and he was proved right. He was mobbed by eligible, intelligent young ladies, but when the boat set sail, there were no more than eleven stalwart women, ranging in age from fifteen to twenty-five, to accompany him back to Seattle.

In Seattle, every man, woman and child turned out to greet the "Mercer Girls." They had a big reception in the common hall and all three pianos in town were put to the gayest use they'd ever seen. By the next spring all but one of the Mercer Girls were married or engaged. Lizzie Ordway remained a spinster, becoming Seattle's first public school teacher and a leader in the Woman's Suffrage Movement.

But eleven women came nowhere near filling the void. So, two years later, Mercer tried again. This time, he got eligible bachelors to contribute to the venture. After arriving in the East, he met General Grant, who offered him a boat to ship his ladies back to Seattle.

Even so, he had difficulty putting his cargo together. He had promised brides to 500 bachelors. It took him no time at all to sign them up. But he hadn't reckoned with James Gordon Bennett. His paper, the *New York Herald*, was the scandal sheet of the times. If they didn't have a story sensational enough, they would make one up. Somehow, Bennett heard about this Mercer fellow from Seattle. He imaginatively reported that Mercer was luring the flower of Eastern womanhood into white slavery – and probably death – in the brothels of Seattle. That did it. Cancellations flooded in. In the end, he sailed with fewer than one hundred brave women.

Another arduous journey around the horn to San Francisco was plagued by lack of funds. When he arrived in San Francisco, he was forced to sell goods purchased for others in Seattle just to get the funds to ship his ladies the rest of the way. This time he could only send them in twos and fives. Even a plea to Governor Pickering of Washington Territory brought no help. Poor Mercer finally got all his girls to Seattle, but what a headache. Again, most were married within the year, but those bachelors who had put up their transport money and were left without a girl were mad as could be. So were the folks who had asked Mercer to buy supplies for them on the East Coast and bring them back with him.

Finally, after marrying one of the girls himself, Mercer left town in disgrace. He settled in Wyoming and became a cattle rancher. It was years later that someone wrote the book called, *Cargo of Brides.* That was turned into a television series "Here Come the Brides" and so the whole affair was romanticized again. Actually, few folks in Seattle ever admit to being a descendant of the Mercer Girls. No one really knows why, except that it seemed to add an air of disgrace to a town that was trying awfully hard to be genteel and refined.

Doc Maynard was still around to remind Seattleites of their origins anyway. He genuinely liked the bottle but, drunk or sober, he had a reputation for honesty and a heart as big as all outdoors. Folks loved to tell the story about Mike Simmons' son (Catherine's nephew) who fell madly in love with a young girl – very young as it turned out. Refused permission to marry by their parents because she was only thirteen, the pair stole away to Seattle and headed straight for Uncle Maynard – he always had a solution.

Even in Washington Territory thirteen was too young to marry. But Doc did have an idea. He printed the number eighteen on two pieces of paper and told the girl to put one in each shoe. After doing that and taking a few good slugs of whiskey, the group trooped over to Judge Bagley's for the ceremony. When asked how old she was, the husband swore she was "over eighteen" – and so she was. Doc was always good for comic relief.

Portland was certainly a genuinely more refined town up to the turn of the century. The downtown business district had lovely brick buildings with cast-iron railings, boasting fluted columns and Corinthian capitals. In 1888, Olin Levi Warner finished his magnificent and elaborate masterpiece, the Skidmore Fountain, to quench the thirst of "men, horses and dogs." It was, and is, one of the finest public monuments in any city.

It was about this same time that residential streets with wide, grassy parks, set with benches and planted with elm trees were set out, creating Portland's unique "Park Blocks" – still one of the most pleasant places to promenade in any city. Italianate villas, Gothic cottages and Empire style houses sat happily side by side.

Portland's prominence was assured by the success of the Oregon Railway and Navigation Company. Henry Villard had arrived in New York from Germany in 1853. He described his arrival: "I was utterly destitute of money, had but a limited supply of wearing apparel and that not suited to the approaching cold season, and I literally did not know a single person in New York or elsewhere in the Eastern States to whom I could apply for help and counsel. To crown all, I could not speak a word of English." He was eighteen years old.

Twenty years later Villard, who had distinguished himself in the fields of teaching and journalism in his adopted land, found himself plunging into a brand new enterprise. Out of a chance meeting in Germany in 1872, Villard agreed to represent the stockholders of the Oregon and California Railroad Company. He visited Oregon in 1874 and was hooked. He immediately saw the potential for profit in railroading and soon made himself president of the new company he called the Oregon Railway and Navigation Company. By 1883, Villard had spent 20,000,000 dollars building over 500 miles of roadbed and could smile in the knowledge that his line was the most profitable in the United States.

Villard had his worries, though. Word had it that the Northern Pacific was planning to terminate its cross-country line in Tacoma, Washington. That would undermine Villard's enterprise. He was committed to Portland. On the other hand, he was also committed to the old adage that "If you can't beat them, join them." So, he devised an alternative scheme. He quietly started buying up Northern Pacific stock. But he needed more money. His credit and word were so good that when he appealed to his Wall Street friends to invest in a project – without revealing what the project was – he was able to raise 8,000,000 dollars. They all called it Villard's "Blind Pool."

By 1881 he was President of the Northern Pacific Railroad Company, and he made Portland his western terminus, connecting it with all his other feeder lines already in place. To please old folks on the Northern Pacific board, he also completed the route North to Tacoma.

One thing you could say for Villard – he had impeccable taste. He was especially fond of the leading U.S. architectural firm of McKim, Mead and White. He had had them build him a magnificent house on Madison Avenue in New York. Now he commissioned them to build a series of railroad stations across the nation, a great contribution to our architectural heritage.

In Portland he decided that it would be great if they designed a hotel for his railway passengers. The 1,000,000-dollar Portland Hotel opened in 1890 and was wonderfully magnificent, with its palm-filled dining room, and its exterior decorated with corner towers, awnings and flowers everywhere. It remained in operation for many years and was finally purchased by the Meier and Frank Company in 1944. In 1952 it was demolished.

Even Villard's railway cars exhibited a very special flair. They contained stained and leaded glass, hand-decorated coffered ceilings and ornate cast-iron transom grilles over the doors.

Railroads meant everything to small, up-and-coming towns like Seattle. What could folks do to compete with Tacoma if they didn't have a railroad? Arthur Denny, his brother David and several new Seattle folk, including Thomas Burke, decided to meet this challenge head on. They organized a railroad of their own and just set about building it. See if they'd let the Northern Pacific get the best of them! They finished it north to the Snohomish River when if finally dawned on the Northern Pacific that these folk were serious. Also, they were stubborn enough to give the Northern Pacific some tough competition.

What happened next is typical of the fiesty folks of Seattle. The Northern Pacific learned about a man in Bellingham who had obtained permission from Congress to construct all the railroad bridges between Seattle and Bellingham, on the North. They bought out his right and sent a lawyer racing to Seattle with a court order requiring that Judge Burke and his cronies halt construction on their bridge over the Snohomish River.

That bridge was critical to the success of the little railroad. Without it, they couldn't reach the coal fields and lucrative freight shipments. Learning in the nick of time about this lawyer, Burke was at the train station when he arrived on his way to Snohomish. What was he to do? Taking the matter in hand, Burke uncoupled the engine from the cars and ordered his engineer to race full steam ahead to Snohomish and "don't even stop at the stations in between." Nobody questioned Judge Burke, so off they went.

As soon as he arrived in Snohomish, the Judge sent the engine back for the rest of the cars (didn't want to lose those fares, you see) while he raced for the courthouse. The sheriff was an old friend. He decided to get the sheriff out of town. He took his deputies to the foothills to look for bandits. By the time the little Northern Pacific lawyer arrived, there was no one to enforce his writ and by the time the possee returned from their bandit hunt, the bridge was completed. That was when the N.P. decided to buy out the little railroad line.

Purchase by the Northern Pacific still didn't guarantee Seattle a cross-country route, though. The Northern Pacific was so angry that this little upstart town had gotten the better of them that for sixteen more years it was impossible for an Easterner to buy a ticket to Seattle. It just didn't appear on any timetable, map or ticket. As far as the N.P. was concerned, Seattle just didn't exist.

Finally, Seattle found their savior in James J. (Jim) Hill. The Northern Pacific had been founded upon land grants from the government. Not so with the emerging Great Northern Railway Company. By cleverly buying several regional lines, and building roadbeds to connect them, and then constructing a brand-new roadbed from Montana west to Everett, Washington, Hill had his railroad – a total of 3,765 miles by 1893.

Best of all for Seattle, Hill really liked the spunky little town. He made it his terminus, thereby forcing the Northern Pacific to extend its line just to compete. Then Hill had a great idea! He unrolled an architect's plans for a tunnel running straight under Seattle with a wonderful, large depot for passengers. This great tunnel and not one, but two, giant depots were completed in 1905. Unlikely as it seems, both the Northern Pacific and the Great Northern ran through it side by side.

Even with all this progress and development, Washington Territory was still just that – a territory. So was Idaho. Completion of the railroad changed all that. No more were the far West territories isolated. Most striking was the population increase the railroads brought. In Washington, the population in 1880 was a mere 75,000; by 1890 that figure was 350,000. It was the same in Idaho. The state could count a population of.32,500 in 1880 and 85,000 in 1890. Montana increased from 40,000 in 1880 to 132,000 in 1890.

As a result of this burgeoning increase in population, Congress finally recognized the pleas of the Western states to be admitted to the Union. Therefore, in November 1889, North Dakota, South Dakota, Montana and Washington were finally admitted to the Union. In 1890, they were followed by Idaho and Wyoming.

1889 was the year of the great fire in Seattle, too. Although Mrs. O'Leary's cow might have started the conflagration in Chicago, it was a boiling glue pot in a cabinet shop that started the Seattle fire. In no time at all the entire town was ablaze. Whistles sounded and bells rang. Shouts of "Fire!" could be heard everywhere. In a city of mostly wooden buildings, the fire spread rapidly. Fire equipment was limited and water pressure low. In fact, it was soon apparent that all the newfangled equipment wasn't of much use at all. They resorted to the old "bucket brigade" method.

The fire raged all afternoon and night. The magnificent Opera House, hotels, the *Seattle Post-Intelligencer*, banks, Yesler's mill, merchant stores – all of downtown – sixty-six blocks of Seattle – was consumed by flames. The *Seattle Post-Intelligencer*, operating from under a tent, but determined to report the greatest story of its existence, said: "Straight to the south with even front moved the terrible wall of flame. Main Street was reached by seven o'clock. The Squire Brick checked the flame only a few moments, then succumbed, adding to the intensity of the scene. The roadways from the buildings all had burned, making escape to the hills difficult.

"In the district south of Yesler Avenue there were more than 150 hotels and lodging houses. The inmates of these places were escaping with their lives and what they wore, and considering themselves fortunate. The Seattle Transfer Company saved its teams and most of its vehicles. South of Yesler Avenue the walls of Schawbacher Brothers, Harrington and Company's brick and stone buildings, and parts of their contents, are now, with the Dexter Horton Bank walls, the only standing monuments to this once busy mart." Estimates of monetary loss were as high as 15,000,000 dollars but, miraculously, no lives were lost.

Did Seattle let a fire slow them down? Not a chance! Instances of unusual enterprise abounded even during the conflagration. One restaurateur saw his business consumed by flames during the first hour. Recognizing that folks would be looking for a good meal when they were hot and tired at the end of the day, he raced up the street and bought out another restaurant, only to have it go up in smoke as well.

Then too, there's the story of the woman who stole a sack of flour in order to provide bread for the hungry firefighters. Imagine her surprise when she took a dozen loaves out of the oven only to find that the sack had contained plaster of paris instead of flour.

While the embers still glowed red, Mayor Moran called a town meeting and plans were laid to rebuild. The new city would be built of brick and stone.

It's this rebuilding of Seattle that gave rise to one of the most unusual phenomena of any city. It's always been said that Seattle is built on seven hills – just like Rome. As romantic as that sounds, for Seattleites that simply meant that getting from one hill to another was difficult, if not almost impossible. For example, Yesler Way (formerly Skid Road) had a 49% grade. Try to get a horse-drawn cart up that, especially in the rain, which was most of the time. The main intersection of downtown, where Pioneer Square is now, was below the water level. Wagons and horses were constantly getting stuck in the mire. It was no joking matter that little ten-year-old Joseph Bufanchio drowned in a chuckhole.

For years merchants and politicians had been scheming about ways to correct this situation. They figured that the best solution was to raise the streets above the tideline. The fire gave them the opportunity. When the rebuilding started in earnest, they simply built buildings with two main floors and two main entrances to them. Business went on an usual on the first floor until the city got around to raising the streets. Then they just filled in the entire first floor and everyone started using the second floor as the main entrance. The original first floor became sort of a basement.

The possibility of access to these elaborate first floors was forgotten about for years until one day John Reddin of the *Seattle Times* wrote an article about it. Everyone laughed and considered it a hoax. Nevertheless, historian and writer Bill Speidel got interested. He started poking around and rather stumbled into a "hidden city." In all honesty, it can't really be claimed that there's much left of the majestic Corinthian pillars, tile floors, marble walls and plaster ceilings that were buried underground. After years of disuse, plaster has crumbled, but brick arches still hint at the old arcades, and some of the cobblestone streets are visible beneath the dirt.

It's possible to take a guided tour through underground Seattle, but be sure to wear old shoes and carry a flashlight or lantern. Most of all, be sure not to miss it.

Portland had its share of fun, too. In 1905, for example, enterprising businessmen dreamed up a way to entice new businesses and visitors to town. They decided to hold an exposition. If Chicago could do it, so could Portland. They called it the Lewis and Clark Centennial Exposition and Oriental Fair and they held it on the 100th anniversary of the arrival of Lewis and Clark.

The Exposition was a wondrous affair, complete with a man-built island and a lake with 1,025 feet of frontage. There was an open-air bandstand where visitors were entertained daily. They added an elaborate *beaux-arts* building called the Agricultural Palace, a U.S. Government Building and a Bridge of Nations connecting the two. The Exposition didn't bring many more settlers to Portland, but those who came enjoyed themselves immensely.

Not to be outdone, Seattle decided to have an exposition of its own. They called theirs the Alaska-Yukon-Pacific Exposition, and they held it in 1909. The University of Washington was located on a forested tract of land virtually out of town, but they decided that was the best spot anyway. It had a distinct drawback, though. State law allows no liquor to be sold within two miles of the University. This was the only fair to ever be held "dry."

The architecture was once again in the flamboyant *beaux-arts* style, complete with lakes, bridges, turrets, cupolas and arches. There were sixty-seven buildings in all.

The Olmsted brothers, designers of Central Park in New York City, were persuaded to do the overall plan for the fair. They created a long pool that descended gently in a series of waterfalls – lit at night from beneath the water. The entire exposition was hailed by reporters from all over the world as the most beautiful ever held. Best of all, some of the buildings remain to grace the present University of Washington campus.

A fair amount of the success of the exposition can be attributed to James Wood, city editor of the *Seattle Times*, who was named "Director of Exploitation" (somehow that does seem more appropriate than Public Relations). He used the paper, and every other method available, to encourage people to come.

The A-Y-P Exposition was a great success. Daily attendance varied from 34,000 to 117,000. A total of 3,740,500 people surged through the gates at various times, bringing a total of 1,096,500 dollars in revenue. Even after expenses there was a 64,000-dollar profit for the backers.

Seattle is fortunate in being able to count not one, but two successful World Fairs in its history. Fifty years later the president of Western International Hotels (now Westin Hotels), Edward Carlson, received a call from Governor Arthur Langlie asking him to become chairman of a new board he had just approved. He called it a World's Fair Commission and Carlson immediately said "Yes."

They decided to hold it on the grounds of the City Center, a complex that housed the high school stadium and an ice arena. Just as with the A-Y-P Exposition, the Seattle World's Fair left behind a magnificent complex known as Seattle Center. It includes the Pacific Science Center, tree-lined promenades, flashing bursts of water from delightful fountains, a refurbished Opera House, lots of green grass for picnics or listening to free music, a Coliseum for sports events and a graceful, revolving restaurant, supported on slender legs, affording diners a spectacular view of mountains, land and sea with their dinner and drinks.

Unlike the A-Y-P the Seattle World's Fair was not "dry."

There was a show street and a gayway and Gracie Hanson's Paradise International featured lovely "topless" ladies in otherwise elaborate costumes. Everyone compared it to those flashy Las Vegas shows. Some say this was proof that Seattle had grown up. Others laughed and said it was proof the Seattle had never left her rowdy, brawly waterfront saloons far behind.

No matter. The Seattle World's Fair was a financial success. Today, even though Gracie Hanson's is no longer around, over seven-and-a-half million people still visit the Seattle Center grounds annually. Some are in jeans to relax on the lawn; others come in black tie to attend an opening at the Opera House. Either way, Seattle Center is still there to provide something for almost everyone.

But that's today. Back in 1903, an event of remarkable proportions occurred in Seattle that was to have a lasting impact on the fledgling city. A young man by the name of William Boeing arrived at the doorstep. He was fresh out of Yale, and restless. Money was no object since his parents had lots, but he did have a problem with a yacht he was trying to build. In order to finish it to his satisfaction, he purchased a shipyard. He loved boats, but when he saw his first airplane, boating everafter took second place.

His first airplane ride was in a flimsy little thing with skinny wings covered with muslin. The pilot took him to the dizzying height of 1,000 feet. That was in 1916. Boeing returned to ground convinced he could build a better airplane than that.

Since he already owned a shipyard, he set about building the wings there. But he also built a shed that housed what is still fondly known as the Big Kite Factory, where he assembled the rest of the plane.

Almost immediately he started building airplanes for the Navy to use in World War I. But before long the war was over. Bill Boeing wasn't sure what to do next. So he built hat racks, telephone booths, umbrella stands and, finally, even bedroom suites. None of these were too profitable, so he went back to airplanes.

In 1919 he launched the first air mail service from Seattle to British Columbia. That venture was so successful that in 1926 Boeing was awarded the air mail route between San Francisco and Chicago. They built a dandy little plane to fly this route. It could carry two passengers and 1,200 pounds of mail. They also formed a dandy little company to operate the new mail routes. They called it Boeing Air Transport. In 1931, Boeing Air Transport joined with three other regional companies to form United Air Lines, a national carrier.

By this time the Big Kite Factory out in Seattle was building a little number called a Model 40 and they wanted to build a long-range bomber for the Army. The Army was mighty interested and the B-17 was born.

How did it get the name "Flying Fortress?" Shortly after the war began, as it turns out on December 14, 1941, right after Pearl Harbor was attacked, an American pilot was separated from his formation in dense fog. Suddenly, he realized that he was surrounded by eighteen Japanese Mitsubishi Zeros.

These deadly little planes were fast and frisky. Like gnats, they seemed to be everywhere at once. The pilot fought gamely but sustained innumerable hits. The radio and tires were blown out. The fuel tank was riddled with bullets, but the plane flew on. Finally, the Zeros turned back. They had run out of ammunition. The American pilot turned back to his base, certain he would never make it.

Somehow, the plane landed and seven very lucky survivors climbed down. Later, President Franklin Roosevelt related the story of the "Flying Fortress" to the American public in one of his fireside chats. The pilot personally came to Seattle to thank Boeing. He addressed the 18,000 Boeing employees saying: "We were just getting onto the knack of shooting them down, when they had to go home. But we survivors and my departed buddies, God rest them, don't get all the credit. For us and a lot of other B-17 outfits I want to thank you for the design and the workmanship in that great plane. Keep it up and we can't lose this war."

But Boeing certainly wasn't sitting around on its laurels. They had been busy designing a brand-new aircraft. They called it the B-29 and the Army bought that too. The B-29 was followed by the B-47, which was followed by entrance into the commercial market. There are 707s and 747s and 727s and 767s – all reliably made by the Big Kite Factory.

A lot of the Pacific Northwest's economy rises and falls with the profitability of Boeing. Back in the 1970s, when the government cancelled the SST program, huge billboards proclaimed: "Would the last person out of Seattle, please turn out the lights?" At least the citizens haven't lost their sense of humor.

By now it's apparent that rugged individualists are the folks most often attracted to the Pacific Northwest. They're the ones not afraid to have an opinion and state it. Doc Maynard is one example. Oregon's ex-governor Tom McCall was another. He was so fiercely protective of the Oregon style of life that he invited Californians to come to visit, but urged them not to stay.

James Beard, probably the foremost authority on American food, was raised in Portland, Oregon, and spent his summers on the Oregon Coast near Gearhart, perfecting his palate. He had written often of his father's breakfasts consisting of freshly caught trout or sautéed chicken with bacon and cream sauce. Also of his mother, who had owned Portland's Gladstone Hotel and taught young Jim to search for nothing but the most perfect Oregon cheddars, Gravenstein apples, greengage plums and Royal-Anne cherries direct from their own trees. The summers spent at the beach picnicking, clamming, fishing, berrying and cooking it all up over a driftwood fire on the beach sound wonderful.

James Beard and most other food connoiseurs will agree that perhaps the finest shellfish anywhere is found right in the deep waters of the Pacific just off the coast of the Western states. Its name conjures visions of succulent, firm, white meat that is sweet and juicy. It was first harvested just out of the little town of Dungeness, Washington, on the Olympic Peninsula. It takes the name of this tiny village as its own.

The only suitable way to eat Dungeness Crab is to chill and crack it very fresh from the water. Natives will tell you that it should be eaten with no sauce at all, but a lightly spiced butter sauce. A mustard-flavoured mayonnaise will do nicely, too. Serve it with a Caesar salad and broiled cheese bread, and with either a dry white wine or beer and it can't be beaten.

Eddie Bauer loves Dungeness crab. Eddie was born in a log cabin on Orcas Island in the San Juan Island chain. His father was a farmer. When Eddie was thirteen years old, the Bauer family moved from Orcas to Seattle. That's when Eddie started working in a sporting goods store. He found that the better service he gave his customers, the more they asked him to serve them. Soon he was in terrific demand.

He learned to make guns and to string tennis rackets. At one time he even showed folks in Seattle how fast he could string them by sitting in the window of the sporting goods store and stringing just as fast as he could. In 1920 he opened Eddie Bauer's Tennis Shop. In his off-hours he went hunting and fishing and enjoyed the great outdoors. He field-tested everything that he sold in his stores. If he couldn't find it to sell, then he just had it manufactured himself.

That's how he happened to be the first to manufacture down-filled outergarments. In 1930 he started importing fancy feathers for his fly-tying business. Then he started using the feathers in a special badminton shuttlecock he invented. One winter after he almost died from exposure to the cold on a fishing trip, he decided to make himself a down-filled jacket. It was lightweight and toasty warm. Pretty soon he was making it for his friends and then for his mail order business. He said: "I started with ten seamstresses. They were knocking them off the year round. From 1936 through 1940, I was just putting money away ass over tea-kettle."

The Second World War interrupted this production line, but although the military requisitioned all the goose down, they asked Bauer to use it to make sleeping bags and flight suits for them. Pretty soon he had over 400 people working on three shifts, seven days a week.

Because of Bauer's insistence on quality, the reputation of his company just kept getting better and better. But as he says: "My greatest contribution to the consumer was our 100 percent, unconditional, lifetime satisfaction guarantee – or your money back, including shipping costs both ways. It was the first and only one of its kind for thirty-five years. That guarantee was part of what I sold."

Today, the Eddie Bauer company continues to be an example of how a young boy can make good. The company produces over eighteen million catalogs a year and now have thirty-one stores across the United States and Canada. They range from Edina, Minnesota, to Palo Alto, California. The main branch is still located in Seattle, recently moving into a new, modern location on the corner of Fifth and Union in Rainer Square.

It's folk like Eddie Bauer who inspired folk like Jack Pennington – that intrepid outdoorsman in the beginning of this tale – to climb the mountains, fish the streams, hunt the fields and forests, to ski the slopes and boat the waterways. It brings families from all over the world to wonder at the majesty of the mountains and marvel at the beauty of the seas. It truly is "God's Country."

Previous page, these pages and overleaf: Harris Beach State Park, Oregon. This still-wild coastline was the much sought for goal of explorers dreaming of a Northwest Passage: that elusive East-West link between the Atlantic and the Pacific. Of course, in order to attain what Hall Jackson Kelley termed "The loveliest ... country on earth" in his 1831 treatise on Oregon, intrepid pioneers had eventually to breach the Rockies.

OREGON

Right: Samuel H. Boardman State Park, Oregon. The romance and, on occasions, turbulence of Oregon's southern coastline has changed relatively little since Captain Vancouver first mapped it, between 1792 and 1794. Nowadays its beaches are a rich resource for beachcombers of international pickings given up by the Pacific Ocean.

OREGON

Facing page: (top) the chalk cliffs of Cape Blanco State Park, and (bottom) Heceta Beach, the view south towards Florence. Above: Yaquina Head Lighthouse, and (overleaf) the sandstone coast of Shore Acres State Park. Oregon's varied landscape seems to confirm the words of William Cullen Bryant: "To him who in the love of Nature holds / Communion with her visible forms, she speaks / A various language."

Crater Lake (left) is, at a depth of 1,932 feet, America's deepest lake, lying within a huge volcanic caldera. It stretches six miles in diameter, and its brilliant indigo color results from the fact that sunlight penetrates up to 400 feet into its waters. The lake formed in the collapsed cone of volcanic Mount Mazama after it erupted 7,000 years ago.

OREGON

Following the eruption 7,000 years ago which formed Crater Lake, further volcanic activity caused Wizard Island (above) to rise above the waters of the lake. Viewing the lake in its winter state (overleaf) it is hard to imagine the immense temperatures, in excess of 3,500°F, generated during its formation. The water that filled the lake and feeds Videa Falls (facing page) has made a tourist attraction of the volcanic mountain, now designated Crater Lake National Park, Oregon's only national park.

The 9,000-foot-high summit of Mount Bachelor (above), made easily accessible by its Summit Chairlift (left), affords a breathtaking view of Oregon's Cascade Lakes area spreading out around and below it. Included in this panorama are the Three Sisters and Broken Top Mountain (top left and overleaf). Central Oregon is famous for smaller rocks too. Thundereggs – Oregon's state rock – agates and other semi-precious stones abound over this area. Volcanic glass and pumice are also to be found – evidence of the volcanic activity that formed much of central Oregon and the lava fields underlying it.

OREGON

Right: South Falls, one of fourteen waterfalls in Silver Falls State Park, lying twenty-nine miles east of Salem, the capital of Oregon. Overleaf: Oregon's Warm Springs River looking rather cold.

OREGON

Right: the Sahalie Falls, and (overleaf) Broken Top Mountain. The rugged terrain of central Oregon can only inspire a great admiration for the people who went west; those who, in the words of Boyd Gibbons, "almost overnight transformed the United States from half a country into half a continent." The drive to get there was, perhaps, at its most extreme in the case of Willie Keil, who was fully determined to see Oregon. He died before he could, but his father, Dr. Keil, who had promised the boy that he would reach Oregon, brought him anyway. In 1855, Willie's body, preserved in alcohol and placed in a zinc casket, reached its destination.

OREGON

The distinctive State Capitol building (right) in Salem, Oregon, is topped with a gold-clad statue of an Oregon pioneer. In the 1850s, Theodore Winthrop, a descendant of John Winthrop of the Massachusetts Bay Colony, described Oregon as being the perfect environment in which to create "new habits of life and thought." It seems appropriate that the descendant of a pilgrim should so describe this land of pioneers. Lewis and Clark's expedition is also commemorated in the murals and statues decorating the State Capitol.

Cannon Beach (left), and Netarts Bay (overleaf), both in northern Oregon, are part of the wild shoreline that the likes of Captain James Cook and Sir Francis Drake found to be a wild and tempestuous prologue to a wilderness land.

Portland city (these pages), Oregon, on the junction of the Willamette (above) and Columbia rivers, sprawls at the feet of Mount St. Helens. As a city, it has managed to retain much of its old character, and it is also known as the City of Roses because it is host to a magnificent annual rose festival. The decision to name the city after Portland, Maine, rather than Boston, Massachusetts, was made on the toss of a coin by two of its early citizens in 1844.

Mount Hood (left), 11,235 feet high and Oregon's tallest mountain, dominates the Cascade Range. According to Indian legend, there was once a natural bridge spanning the Hood River at Cascade Locks near Bonneville. The bridge was flung into the water by Tyhee Sahale, the Supreme Being, when infuriated by the fight his two sons were having over the beautiful guardian of the bridge's sacred flame. The resultant debris created the river's cascades, and the three lovers involved were resurrected as Mount Hood, Mount Adams and Mount St. Helens.

Above: Wahkeena Falls in the Cascade Range, Mount Hood National Forest. Legend has it that a great sickness once afflicted the Multnomah people, and an old medicine man told them that the only means to end the affliction was the sacrifice of a maiden who would throw herself from the high cliff of Multnomah Falls (facing page) on the Columbia River to the rocks below. When the Chief's daughter saw the sickness take hold of her lover, she went to the cliff of Oregon's highest fall and threw herself to her death. Apparently, when a breeze blows through the falls, a stream separates out from it in the form of a woman, indicating the Great Spirit's acceptance of her sacrifice.

Not all the waterways formed in the Columbia River Gorge are as dramatic as the Latourell Falls (left). The waters of Oneonta Gorge (overleaf) are placid and as clear as glass.

WASHINGTON

Washington, the Evergreen State, exhibits an almost bewildering variety of landscapes. Perhaps a suitable Washingtonian catchphrase would be to adopt the cartoonist Walt Kelley's maxim: "We have looked at nature, and it is us." Nowhere is man's interaction with nature more obvious than over the gently swelling fields of wheat and well-tended agricultural land in the fertile Palouse farming country (right).

The Coulee Dam (above) on the Columbia River, Washington State, is the world's largest gravity-type concrete dam – a man-made spectacle, in complete contrast to the Palouse Falls (facing page), one of nature's splendid creations. Here the Palouse River (overleaf) cascades down to continue its sinuous journey through canyon walls on towards the point where it meets the Snake River.

Mirrored in the waters of Lake Takhlakh, the volcanic peak of southern Washington's Mount Adams (left) towers out of the Washington Cascades.

WASHINGTON

Right: a waterfall plays by Spirit Lake in southern Washington's Gifford Pinchot National Forest.

On the western edge of the Pinchot Forest stands one of the most beautiful peaks of Washington's Cascade Mountains. Mount St. Helens (above), seen before May 1980 looking deceptively serene, suddenly erupted with an earthshaking roar on May 18, 1980, devastating 150 square miles of forest and giving the world spectacular dust-laden sunsets for months afterwards. The bleak aftermath of this explosion at Spirit Lake (facing page), lying at the foot of the mountain, keeps the volcanic nature of the Pacific Northwest dramatically in mind.

WASHINGTON

In Washington's Mount Rainier National Park, the lower reaches of Mount Rainier (right), looking quite alpine, are carpeted with flowers that seem to reflect the blue of the sky. Mount Rainier is the most massive peak in the Cascades. A few peaks are officially taller, but none can compare with Mount Rainier's twenty-six glaciers, comprising the largest single peak system in the continental United States.

In the area (overleaf) around Paradise, in Mount Rainier National Park (these pages and overleaf), one can see the peaks of Mount Rainier, wander through shaded groves such as the Grove of the Patriarchs (above), and gaze on Falls Creek (facing page) as it spreads like a bridal veil over the rocks.

Mount Shuksan (left and overleaf), part of Washington's North Cascades, towers over the waters of Picture Lake. This area was subject to a gold rush in 1858, but the boom was short-lived, lasting only a year, owing to the hardships caused by the landscape and the difficulty of gaining access to the area. The barely restrained power of the Cascades' mountain climate is easily glimpsed in the swift mood swings of the weather. One small dark cloud and the mountain seems to lower ominously.

Glacier Peak Wilderness (left) in the North Cascades of Washington State holds some spectacular glaciated peaks – the most remarkable of which is Glacier Peak itself (overleaf).

WASHINGTON

Washington's largest city, Seattle (right and overleaf) is hemmed in by mountains, including the great bulk of Mount Rainier. The state's motto is Alki, "By and By," but the modernity and bustle of Seattle, dominated by its 600-foot-tall Space Needle (left), seems to belie the implied leisureliness of these words.

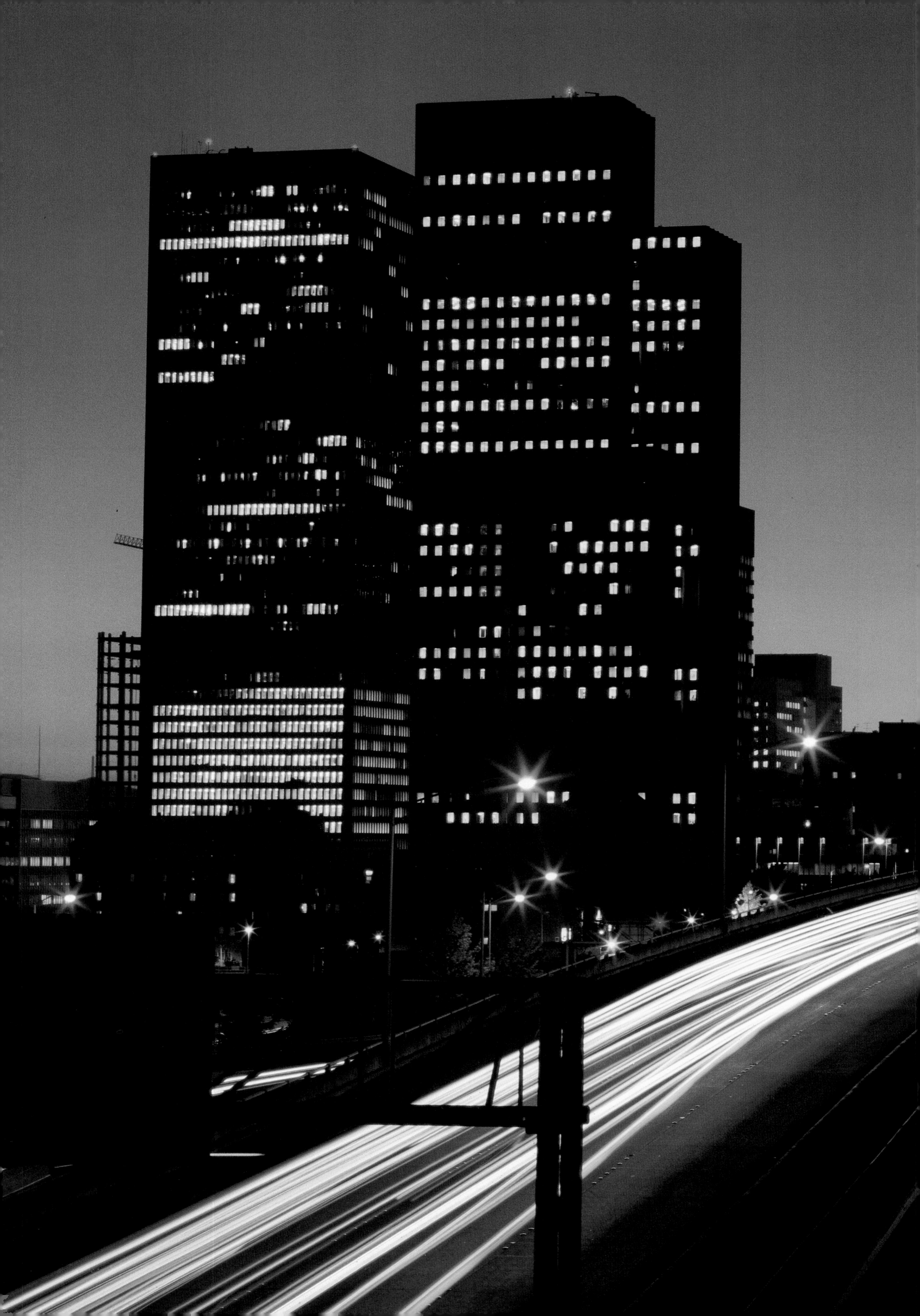

The slender, almost tenuous form of Seattle's Space Needle (facing page) dominates the city's downtown area. From it the regimented rows of sailing boats (above), anchored in a harbor fed by Puget Sound, are clearly visible. Great Bend (overleaf) on the Hood Canal threads along the eastern edge of the Olympic Peninsula, across the Sound from Seattle. Lit by the evening's golden sun at the feet of the Olympic Mountains, placid Hood Canal is in complete contrast with Seattle's urban sprawl.

The Pacific Northwest is most particularly famed
for beaches pounded by the restless Pacific.
Isolated Rialto Beach (left) lies seventeen miles
south of Cape Alava, at the northern tip of
Olympic National Park's coastal strip.

Washington State offers an immense variety of landscapes, many of which can be explored within the Olympic Peninsula (these pages and overleaf) alone Facing page: (top) Grayland Beach, and (bottom) the coastline at Queets, in Olympic National Park. Lumber is frequently tossed up onto the Pacific shores. Below: Crescent Lake, and (overleaf) the Hall of Mosses in the dense rainforest of the Coast Range.

Extending northward into British Columbia, Canada, the Pacific coastline becomes part of Pacific Rim National Park, in which beautiful seascapes, such as those at Green Point (left), are protected.

From the southernmost point of Broken Group Islands (above and right) one can see Vancouver Island in the background. This part of British Columbia is rich in wildlife, particularly tidal-feeding gulls (top right), which clamor in the peace of Pacific Rim National Park (these pages and overleaf). Overleaf: dawn over South Beach and its driftwood debris.

Above: yachts, bristling with masts, collect in Victoria's harbor, overlooked by the Parliament Buildings, in readiness for the annual "Swift Sure" yacht race. Victoria's Butchart Gardens (left and top left) lie on a site once occupied by a cement plant. In 1904, Mr. Robert Pim Butchart and his wife began its transformation into the series of gardens there today. Horseshoe Bay (overleaf) serves as a scenic ferry port for travelers to Vancouver Island.

Vancouver city (these pages and overleaf) was once a sawmilling settlement named Granville. It was renamed after Captain George Vancouver of the British Royal Navy, who had navigated the coast in 1792. It is still a city for sailing enthusiasts, with many boats and yachts moored in its inlets and harbors. These days the city favors all forms of transportation. The Lions Gate Bridge (above) was built to provide easy access across the Burrard Inlet to the new development of West and North Vancouver.

BRITISH COLUMBIA

Lakes, such as Pavilion Lake (right), near Lillooet, afford British Columbians excellent water-sport opportunities, and man-made amendments to the land create spring-blossoming orchards in the Okanagan Valley (overleaf).

Passengers on the Prince George *(left) can take the "Inside Passage" trip, which passes by jagged mountains (top left) in ice-strewn waters, and view the massive bulk of the glacier at Tracy's Arm (above) from close quarters. The mountains of British Columbia are quite spectacular, as is evidenced by the Bishop Glacier (overleaf) near the Lillooet Valley, and mountains (following page) near the west coast of Vancouver Island.*